DIVINE STATE OF MIND®

THE GATEWAY TO FINDING ANSWERS FROM WITHIN

Joyfully,

Susan Lawrence

Table of Contents

DEDICATION

I dedicate this book to my Mom, Gloria DeCola, affectionately known as Momma Gloria. She taught me to embrace all things spiritual, from astrology to the Akashic Records and everything in-between. I hope I have made her proud . . .

I miss you Mom.

ACKNOWLEDGMENTS

I wish to thank the following people for their tremendous support, time, and love:

My father, Joseph DeCola, whose wise words "things change" helped me navigate the arduous chapters of my life. His love, compassion, and non-judgment have enhanced my journey through this life. And Yes Dad, there is life after death!

 My sister, Lorraine McGrath, whose love and encouragement lead me to write this book.

My children, Maria Cashion and Stephanie Maillard, and beautiful grandchild, Lena Cashion, who brighten my days.

My dear friend, Joanne Wood, who has supported and encouraged me for over 47 years. Susan Farmer and Lynne Barnett, who enrich my life with humor and laughter.

My friends, Connie Fox and Sonja Bednar, for their enlightenment and deep spiritual connections.

To Katie, for the endless hours spent transcribing the sessions which have created this book.

Dr. Brian Weiss, for opening my eyes to the possibilities of deeper healing through hypnosis, Past Life Regressions, and so much more.

To all of my clients, who graciously gave me permission to record and share their stories with my readers.

A special thank you to my husband, Peter, who spent countless hours behind the scenes supporting me from start to finish. Your help was truly a labor of love. I couldn't have done this without you.

And finally, I express my loving gratitude to God, Jesus, Source, Mother Mary, Archangels Michael and Gabriel, and the Consciousness of all the deceased loved ones, who generously offered love and healing to my clients.

PREFACE

"Down through the shadows of millions of yesterdays
flow the waters of a life everlasting."
~The Eternals, The Journey Within
by Henry Leo Bolduc

I wanted to start this book with a quote from the Eternals who are Higher Spiritual Beings documented to have been channeled through a human "vessel." It is the belief in these words that started me on a journey to learn more about the shadows of yesterdays and how they affect a person's life everlasting. I never dreamed I would I become a spiritual hypnotist, but I will say that my core beliefs led me down a remarkable path for over twenty years.

Ultimately, it led me to the work that I do today. It all began listening to my mother who was an amazing astrologer and extremely well read on numerous related topics. I followed in her footsteps and became an avid reader on the subject of spirituality and other planes of existence. Very often, I consulted with psychic mediums (a living person who communicates with the spirit realm) to help me navigate my life. Whenever I encountered crossroads in my life and felt I needed direction or answers, I would consult with a psychic medium. Curiously, I received many puzzling messages that left me baffled. Huh? What should I do? Where do I go from here? I was never quite sure.

Then one dismal day, when the weather looked like I felt, I decided to explore a bit further, so I contacted a channeler.

When a person channels, they allow a non-physical entity to enter their body for the purpose of communicating with other physical beings. The channeler acts purely as a portal and is not conscious of the information that comes through. That was just what I needed: unfiltered information.

So, I began my search for a channeler and the universe led me to "Veronica." Veronica, as I subsequently learned, is a spirit channeled by a woman named April Crawford. April is a true deep trance / full body spiritual channeler and medium. I arranged a phone session with April to ask for guidance from Veronica. My life was clearly at a crossroads, and I felt lost and uncertain about the future. I waited on the other end of the phone for April to channel Veronica. I had no idea what to expect, and I was nervous about the message that I would receive.

A few minutes into the phone call, April had made contact with Veronica. "You should be a life coach," Veronica suggested. A life what? I had no knowledge of what a life coach was. The session continued, and I wrote down the words "Life Coach" on a notepad to help me remember to do some research on the subject after the phone call ended.

Since I was completely unfamiliar with the term 'life coach', I decided to research it using the Internet. I learned that a life coach is someone trained to help improve another's personal or professional life by using NLP (Neuro Linguistic Programing) and other techniques designed to help them reach their goals. It sounded interesting to me, so I continued with my research to learn more about NLP and life coaching. I enrolled in a class to become a certified life coach, NLP practitioner, and clinical hypnotist/hypnotherapist. I found the course material very intriguing and one day following a lesson on hypnosis, it was time to practice.

Everyone in the class wanted to be hypnotized, and interestingly enough, no one but me wanted to perform the role of the hypnotist. So I eagerly volunteered to test my newly learned skills and hypnotized the entire class in a single session. I was astonished by the results, and I became instantly hooked. The technique for performing hypnosis resonated so well with me that I became even more eager to learn. I learned how to help people stop smoking, lose weight, and release fears and phobias. The focus of my early practice was centered primarily on these core competencies.

But shortly after that, the real fun began. I started focusing on regression therapy. Regression therapy is a hypnotic technique that takes a person back to their early childhood in search of repressed memories that may have left them with limiting beliefs that now challenge the person in an adverse way. I'll talk more about limiting beliefs later in the book. Regression Therapy also focuses on going back (in terms of memory) in time into the womb, in vitro.

The ability to learn about a person's experience inside the womb was so intriguing and enlightening that I found myself wanting to know more. So, what happens before we enter the womb? My mother also taught me that we choose our parents prior to being born. Through my experience as a Clinical Hypnotist, I've learned that my mother was right; we do choose our parents. Most often, we need certain people to help us fulfill our life's plan and to balance karmic ties.

That means if you do something helpful or hurtful to someone else in one lifetime, there must be a balancing of that energy either in the same lifetime or perhaps in another. So while in vitro regressions were interesting and informative, it seemed necessary in many cases to go further back and take a deeper dive, if you will, into a client's consciousness.

Perhaps a past lifetime would hold the key to resolving the issues being experienced in this lifetime. Dr. Brian Weiss wrote many books on the subject of past life regression including Many Lives, Many Masters, and he brought this practice to the forefront. He is the world's foremost expert on the subject of past-life regression therapy, and I met him at Omega while attending a course on past life regression. He explained that while a person is in a very relaxed state of hypnosis, their mind is capable of remembering everything since their conception.

Conception may be from this lifetime or previous ones transcending back to the birth of the soul. What is most intriguing to me during sessions with my clients is their ability to articulate such detail about whom they were, as well as when and where they lived. Obscure details such as specific place and time, their dress, family members, and similar evidence are often revealed during past life regressions. The most startling coincidences are discovered during past life regressions involving people with whom clients have relationships in the present lifetime; people who obviously do not look the same, but have incarnated as a different person.

Their relationship in the previous lifetime is one that perhaps created the underlying issue that now persists in the present lifetime. The significant aspect is what may have happened between the two during that past lifetime. Did they love each other or were they rivals? Did one die and leave the other heartbroken? Perhaps one killed the other in a bitter dispute? The information is fascinating and at the same time extremely healing. These are some of the stories I will reveal to you later in this book. My journey didn't stop there, and I wanted more. I wanted my clients to be able to access their consciousness and find answers for themselves. I wanted them to discover their dharmic path to enjoy the fullness of life. I knew of the Akashic Records from my mother.

The Akashic records, as she explained, contain a permanent record of your life and every person's life. The records contain all the details of a person's karma. These records exist in another dimension. But they are yours, and you always have access to them. It is your divine right to use them. In The Journey Within written by Henry Leo Bolduc, his friend or the "vessel" channeled the "entities." Their account of the records is stated eloquently.

According to Leo Bolduc, the Akashic Records are the "...permanent records of life, the permanent records of life that are kept of every act and deed, of all history and of all thought of all medicine and technology, of all advancements, are kept in your own consciousness and the consciousness of every individual. Therefore, if you look deep within, you will see all that exists, that has existed and will exist. This is hidden in the recesses of your mind. You must be willing to accept yourself and to look deep within your own mind, and then you will see and understand and perceive this."

With this revelation, I began searching for the perfect hypnotic trance that people could use all around the world to view their own Akashic Records. My journey took another interesting turn while my clients were visiting the Akashic Library. It became evident that when my clients entered into their superconscious mind, they were able to access All-There-Is and communicate directly with Source to receive messages and healings. And so with my husband, family, and friends by my side, I began an exciting, inspiring, and enlightening adventure!

INTRODUCTION

"We are all psychics, and we are all Gurus.
We have merely forgotten."
~ Dr. Brian Weiss, Only Love is Real

I believe that the idea of unconscious, conscious, subconscious, and superconscious minds may be obscure for many people. So whenever I see a new client, I like to teach him or her how hypnosis works, why it works and how it feels. I explain all this by using a metaphor. Our minds love images, and I have found that this particular metaphor works well to introduce the concept. Following, is a typical conversation I had recorded with a new client during the introductory phase.

"I would like you to picture your mind in four parts," I began.

"My mind in four parts?" questioned my client.

"Yes. Can you imagine that?" I questioned.

"Okay," he agreed.

"So, picture your mind. There are four parts to it. The first part is the unconscious part of your mind, and that unconscious part of your mind is the part that is performing all the behind the scenes work, known in medical terms as involuntary bodily functions. It keeps your heart beating, your respiration going, your eyes blinking, etc., etc. So Let's call it the control room, okay?"

"--Got you—." he said.

"Everything— and you understand as well as I do that when you're unconscious, your body is still functioning."

"Yeah, functioning well actually," he added.

"Yes, functioning very well. We leave that part of your mind alone so you won't need to worry that when you leave here and your phone rings, you don't start clucking like a chicken. I charge extra for that!" I joked to build rapport.

"—Yeah—," he smiled, beginning to relax more.

"Then there's the conscious part of your mind, and I like to describe that as the office. And you are the manager of the office. You sit in the office chair from the age of eight or nine when your critical mind develops."

"Okay," he responded as he was following along.

"All right? So, you're sitting in the office and for everything that's transpiring, you're making a judgment about, right?" I asked.

"Yeah."

"Okay? So you're analyzing everything — this is good, this is bad, this is true, and this is false, this is right, this is wrong, for whatever it is that's transpiring. Now, imagine all of the things you experience on a given day — what you're seeing, you're feeling, you're believing, you're thinking, all of the people you see, all of the things you hear, all of the things you taste. Everything that occurs gets filed in the filing cabinet. Got that?" I questioned.

"Okay."

"So, your office filing cabinet is steadily filling up with all of your thoughts, all of your beliefs, all of your fears, all of your worries, etc.," I continued.

"Got it."

"Now we both know that drawers in a filing cabinet eventually fill up," I explained. "And since there's no trash can in this office, nothing can be thrown out. So, now you are forced to clean out these drawers to make room for more new experiences. So, you take all the stuff in these drawers that you are not using and transfer it to another filing cabinet in a different room. We will call this the file cabinet room."

"The file cabinet room?" he asked.

"Yes. A large storage room designed for files that are not as relevant or required on a minute-to-minute basis. This is what your subconscious mind represents. It is in simple terms a very large room, with many large file cabinets and has virtually unlimited storage for items that are not currently needed. Can you imagine that?" I continued.

"—Yes--." he said nodding his head.

"--There is nothing but files and file cabinets inside this room. No one is in there. There's no judgment in there. It doesn't care if it's right or wrong, or true or false, real or fake; it doesn't matter," I emphasized this very important point.

"Yeah, sure," he responded.

"Now this room is not only large, but it is very organized, and everything is stored there since your inception. It might be from this lifetime, or it could be from a previous lifetime or the lifetime before that, since the conception of your soul. It is so organized that you can access information stored there instantaneously. To illustrate my point, I am going to have you access it right now. While you are consciously aware of what's going on right now, I want you to think of an elephant. Can you bring up an image of an elephant in your mind?" I questioned.

"Yeah."

"Now, how did that happen? Well, because at a specific point in your life you learned about an elephant. You may have drawn an elephant, you may have seen an elephant, you may have heard an elephant, or you may have colored an elephant—"

"—Sure—"

"—You may have ridden an elephant, you may have fed an elephant," I continued.

"—I did ride an elephant," he answered.

"Oh, there you go. So, all those memories of an elephant went right into the filing cabinet under "E" for "elephant." And because you can't be in your office at the same time with a huge elephant roaming around, your subconscious mind with its extraordinary filing system retrieved the image instantaneously for you. You didn't even have to type in the words, and it's faster than Google! So, now I want you to — with your conscious mind, take that elephant and turn him pink. You can do that with your creative mind, can't you," I asked.

"Yeah, I got a pink elephant I can see it," he answered.

"You can see a pink elephant—"

"—in Africa," he interrupted.

"Good. Now add white polka dots?" I requested.

"The same scene I saw, but now he's pink, and he has white polka dots on him," he smiled.

"Great, now add a blue bow on his tail and a funny looking hat on his head. Got it? Now even thought the pink elephant is not real, it gets filed in your subconscious mind right along with the other elephants, right?"

"Okay, I follow," he added.

"I promise you within ten minutes you will not be thinking of an elephant, but the next time you think of an elephant, guess which elephant is going to appear?"

"The pink elephant with the blue bow on its tail and the funny hat!" He answered.

"Right, because it feels better. It makes you laugh. So, when we visit a memory, a childhood memory, a past life memory, or a memory that's upsetting, we can alter it with your conscious mind just like we changed the elephant and re-file it. The subconscious mind doesn't know if it's real or fake and doesn't really care. It just is. So, what we do with hypnosis is relax you so much, where the manager (critical mind) goes to sleep in the office, and we sneak into the file cabinet room and we manipulate the files just like we manipulated the file of the elephant. Do you see how this works?" I asked.

"I do."

"Any limiting belief you have, can be change with hypnosis simply by changing the scene," I continued to explain.

"I like that. But I have one question. What happens before we are eight or nine, and our manager isn't in the office chair yet? What happens then?" He asked.

"Good question. Well, unfortunately, before the age of eight or nine when our minds are not yet developed enough to be critical or analytical then everything we think or feel, whether it be right or wrong, simply gets stored in the subconscious mind as the truth. This is how limited beliefs are born. Let me explain. Pretend it's your first day of school and you are on the playground having a good time. A fifth-grade bully runs past you, knocks you down, and says, 'Move out of the way, Stupid.' Now you have fallen, and you have become emotional. You heard the word stupid, and since it was tied to an emotion, it becomes a limiting belief. The word 'limiting' is used because being or feeling 'stupid' would certainly hold someone back, or limit his or her capability in certain situations. Now ten minutes later, one forgets all about it, but the belief is now an experience hiding in the subconscious mind. Through hypnosis, those limiting beliefs can be found, and a new positive belief can replace it to allow the person to release that feeling. It follows the same analogy as the pink elephant," I explained.

"I get it. I can see that. What's the forth part?" he wondered.

"That's the CEO upstairs. It is the superconscious mind that allows you to experience the spiritual side of things. It's what I call the Divine State of Mind."

In the superconscious mind, one can journey into a supernatural state and encounter spiritual entities beyond this realm. My work with clients begins by visiting a garden where they often meet spiritual beings or loved ones who have passed on. It is very healing to see and speak to loved ones and know that they are very much alive and well, happy and joyful, and watching over you. In the Divine State of Mind, they meet you in the garden to offer love, advice or to help you release some guilt you may be carrying as a result of their death. It is cathartic to release the guilt, pain, and shame and to know they are still with you. Often, they too, need to apologize to you for their behavior and ask for your forgiveness. Sometimes it is mutual, but either way it is very healing.

It is evident from my work that whatever emotional pain, grief, regret, or worry that a person may suffer from, there are modes of therapy using hypnosis that can release patterns of behavior that stifle the human spirit. The evils people battle with daily can be transformed through their superconscious mind as they discover their own answers from within. It is also from within that we each discover and learn how to feel love, compassion, and non-judgment.

The stories I am about to tell are recorded from clients who gave me permission to share their stories with others for the purpose of learning and possibly gaining a better understanding of their own situations. It is not easy to speak while in a deep hypnotic trance, so their sentences are relatively short with long pauses in between. I purposely left out the ellipses to condense their conversations.

This is my journey into finding the gateway to uncovering answers from within. Our souls have access to all knowledge; we just need a way to reach it. This is the gateway to what I now call the Divine State of Mind. The phrase was offered to me by one of my clients who, during a wonderfully hypnotic experience, did not wish to come out of his 'Divine State of Mind.' And so the phrase was coined.

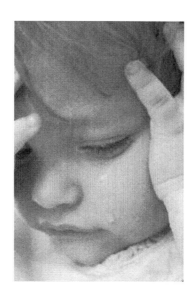

Ouch!

"When we run, hide and try to deny our trauma, the little boy or girl within comes back to seek validation, healing and peace."

~ Cecibel Contreras

"Ouch, you're hurting me..."

I waited for my client to continue.

"You're hurting me Uncle Bob. Please stop...Make him stop! Why is he doing this to me?"

I didn't have an answer yet, and the client didn't seem to be in too much distress. I waited and just listened.

"I must be a bad girl. I must have done something wrong. I'm not a good girl. He's hurting me."

Through hypnosis, my client and I learned about what Uncle Bob did and how his actions were still affecting my client's everyday life. There are many revelations such as these in my work.

Memories like these are often blocked by the conscious mind. They're buried alive in the subconscious, the part of the brain that holds all of our memories from conception (and perhaps even before conception) to the present moment. The revelation above was a memory buried deep in the subconscious mind of a 55-year-old woman who came to me for help with weight loss.

"No matter what I do, I can't lose this weight. I exercise, eat right, watch my portions and still this weight won't come off," she complained during her initial consultation. She had no idea that there could be limiting beliefs that were causing her to hold onto that weight. Through hypnosis, we learned where those beliefs came from so that she could release her protective shield, her weight.

Limiting beliefs that are hidden deep in the subconscious mind can impact our day-to-day lives. Memories that exist beyond our awareness can hold us back. We hold onto these memories and react to them unconsciously without acknowledging them.

Why was this woman holding on to all this weight? As a clinical hypnotist, I had to consider the symbolism behind her struggle.

Could the extra pounds be functioning as a protective shield? Perhaps.

During regression therapy, a form of hypnotherapy, we can unlock the human mind and allow the deep-seated fears, hurtful memories, and limiting beliefs to be exhumed. Just as a scientist discovers ancient secrets by unearthing artifacts and skeletons in the earth, the hypnotherapist can unearth memories and forged beliefs. It is similar to the adage, what skeletons are hiding in your closet? But in terms of hypnosis and hypnotherapy the question becomes, what skeletons are hiding in your past?

When I guide someone into a regressed state, I never know where that client will take me. Let's consider Samantha's situation. She came to me because she wanted to lose weight.

During the initial consultation, where I perform an assessment process with my clients to learn more about them, it was apparent to me that Samantha knew how to respond to my questions. However, I instinctively knew that there was something critical that she wasn't verbalizing. She wasn't even consciously aware of it.

We began the regression in the same way that I perform all relaxing meditation inductions. I guided Samantha through the process of relaxing each part of her body and quieting her conscious mind. This is a slow and methodical process that utilizes guided imagery of walking down to a beach to increase the depth of one's hypnotic trance.

Once Samantha reached a theta stage of trance, which is a deep level of focused relaxation (similar to a dozing off right before sleep), it was easy to access her subconscious mind. Samantha reached this level of consciousness with ease. Once I was confident that she was in a deep trance, I began to guide her through a hypnotic reverie designed to help her access the subconscious and better understand her weight problems.

As Samantha relaxed deeply, I asked her to imagine herself going into a room that held all the positive parts of her; all the parts of her that made her proud of herself. Parts such as compassion, understanding, sympathy, and intelligence. She acknowledged seeing these parts of herself and then we continued.

We had to find the part of her that was hiding. It was a part of her that wanted to remain hidden to continue to hold onto her extra weight. This part of Samantha was afraid to show itself. It hid in a closet, refusing to come out.

With coaxing, she was able to speak to this part of her that normally stays hidden just outside of Samantha's conscious awareness.

Inside the closet, Samantha visualized a key. Keys are metaphorically used for unlocking things that are hiding in one's subconscious mind. Samantha was amazed that she was actually able to see this key and wondered what it was for.

"What does it unlock?" she asked.

"The Truth," it answered.

"The Truth about what?" Samantha asked.

Four shadows appeared.

I encouraged Samantha to ask the shadows what they wanted, and suddenly, Samantha regressed to a time when she was a young girl.

"I'm going fishing with my uncle. We are driving in the car. It is just the two of us." And then, she scowled, "Why isn't my brother here?"

Samantha's uncle left the road and drove towards an abandoned building. "It looks like it used to be a factory or something like that. There is water near the factory. He is making me believe we are going to go fishing in the water. But there are no fish," she said. "And the water is brown . . . It doesn't look like we can fish here."

Samantha wondered out loud why they were at the pond. She didn't understand what was happening. "He is touching my leg. He is telling me that I should be a good girl and listen to him. His hand is going higher and higher up my thigh. He's pushing his hand into my vagina. Ouch! He is hurting me!"

Samantha was feeling deep emotional and physical pain as her uncle continued to molest her. While she was experiencing the emotions, I wanted to know what she was thinking as this would become her limiting belief.

"I'm bad," she responded to my question. "I must be bad. I must have done something wrong. I didn't do something right. I didn't do it right! I'm gonna get in trouble. I'm a bad girl."

Samantha assumed that she must be bad. She believed that she had done something very wrong to be hurt in this way by her uncle.

The child's young view of being molested was to think that she was the one who was bad. She was the one who did something wrong. When a thought occurs at the same instant an emotional response does, the two become linked together as a limiting belief.

It is limiting because in this case the idea of being 'bad' or 'not doing it right' limited her confidence about herself. When limiting beliefs are too painful to remember, the subconscious mind hides them. But beliefs always look for validation. Even though they're hidden, these beliefs still make themselves known in our daily lives.

Years after this incident, Samantha continued to hold onto the belief that she was 'not doing it right.' Every poor decision she made and every wrong answer entered on a test validated this hidden limiting belief.

The conscious mind, which is the part of our mind that we're aware of during our waking hours, has no knowledge that there are subconscious beliefs operating behind-the-scenes. We may consciously feel stirrings somewhere in the mind, body or heart, but remain blissfully unaware of their true meaning. Healing the inner child is the most important part of the regression therapy. By having Samantha imagine herself as she is now made her feel strong. She could see that she was 'doing things right.'

Now it was time to begin the healing process. Imagining herself as she is now looking down from above the scene with her uncle, Samantha took the little girl and carried her away.

I asked Samantha, "Wouldn't it be nice if you had known then everything that you know now? Tell the little you what you would want her to know from your perspective as an adult."

I paused and allowed Samantha to speak with her inner child. "Tell the little you how she is not bad. How it is not her fault. That she did everything right."

Samantha wept as I continued, "Tell her that she no longer has to worry about that uncle. She is safe now. Tell her everything in your heart. Tell her that she is loved. Truly loved. Give her all the insight and knowledge you have about life now that you're an adult. Tell her how wonderful she is and what a beautiful woman she will be and how she is very worthy."

A new look came over Samantha's face, as she inwardly conveyed these messages to her inner child. I asked her to give her little self a special hug. The best hug she could ever image.

I asked Samantha to imagine absorbing that little girl back into herself. She took some time to imagine this process and I was very patient as she absorbed the inner child completely.

Then, it was time for Samantha to come back to waking consciousness. I counted her back slowly until she was ready to open her eyes.

It was hard for Samantha to believe what she had just experienced. She had many questions:

Why did her parents allow her to be alone with her uncle? Why did they go to that pond? Didn't her parents think it was strange for their daughter to go fishing alone with her uncle?

We talked about the times when people rarely worried about things like incest, kidnappings, and molestations. It was a time of trust. Mothers would leave their babies in carriages outside the store. These were different times. We concluded our session and weeks later I received this email from Samantha:

"I have been reflecting a lot, and it has given me perspective on some of my life choices. I have been journaling a bit, and I've made a list of some other instances that will probably explain the other shadow figures. I am not hesitant to dig into this, but I don't know what to do with it now? I pose this question and answer it as well. I think the truth is good. I also think everyone has some sort of abuse in their background either physical, mental or emotional. It is so common. What does still surprise me though, is that I had no idea it happened so young. Nurturing my inner child was a really good experience. I heal when I go there and I think of it. Thank you. I have really appreciated our relationship."

A subsequent email explained how her younger sister had a strange, vague memory of a similar sort. Not surprising as it is common when family members are involved. Unlocking the secrets of the past is a huge "weight" off of Samantha's shoulders (and waistline) now. She is free to enjoy her life.

School Daze

"It takes so little to make a child happy, that it is a pity in a world full of sunshine and pleasant things, that there should be any wistful faces, empty hands, or lonely little hearts."

~ Louisa May Alcott, Little Men Little Women, #2

I had seen Steve twice before. The first time we met, he sought my help because he wanted to have more joy in his life. When I asked him to explain exactly what he meant by that, his answer revealed that he felt unappreciated and uncomfortable in social situations. Specifically, he felt uncomfortable speaking up to authority figures. He also wanted more "Me

Time." "Me Time" to Steve was simply to sit on the beach alone or be with his wife.

I took notes and carefully considered Steve's situation. I looked up from my notepad and Steve took a deep breath. It was difficult for him to say this:

"I want to be more assertive."

Then it was clear. I understood the connection between assertiveness and joy.

"What I have to say doesn't seem important," he explained. Steve's lack of self-confidence was very obvious at this point, but I still wanted to understand his situation better. I decided to perform a childhood regression so that we might learn more about what was going on in his subconscious mind.

We began the regression in the usual way. I guided Steve into a state of deep but focused relaxation. I used guided imagery and listened carefully to find out more about Steve's situation from the perspective of his subconscious mind.

During the regression, Steve immediately went to a childhood memory of his school days. According to this memory, much of his free time was spent helping the librarian. Steve was afraid to go outside and play with the other children. He remembered binding the books, organizing the shelves and doing the "daily stuff." He had no distinct memory of being bullied during this period, but he knew someplace deep down that something important had happened. We went deeper, further into his past into the earlier years.

It was during these early school days before being with the librarian that Steve lost his confidence to speak up. Children can be cruel; we all know that, and their verbal attacks can cause lifelong limiting beliefs.

"I'm in the play park. It's my first day at primary school. I am very excited. A boy older than I, he looks like he could be in junior school comes over to me. I am waiting to play cricket. One boy won't let me. Said I was too little. I told him I was not, and he said, 'move out of the way, stupid' and pushed me down. I cried."

As I have explained in the introduction, this is how a limiting belief is born. Steve had an experience insofar as he was pushed down, and it hurt his bottom and his pride. At the same time, he heard the word, stupid. A young child has no critical thought process in his head before the age of eight. In other words, there is no judgment about the situation or the word that he heard. At that age, we are incapable of decreeing for ourselves that the bigger boy was just a bully and had no real idea of Steve's intelligence. However, when an emotion is tied to a thought, it becomes a limiting belief. (Emotional pain + hearing or thinking the word 'stupid' = a limiting belief) Limiting beliefs manifest themselves when a similar situation, thought or feeling occurs.

Steve had learned early on that he would be chastised for speaking up, and those beliefs were holding him back as an adult. We reframed the memory for Steve. Since our subconscious mind does not know the difference between what is real and what is not, we re-created the scene. Steve now had a new image of himself speaking up to people. He envisioned himself standing up to the bully and watched the bully back down and let him play cricket. He even watched himself become an all-rounder, a player who performs well at both batting and bowling. The image gave him a chuckle.

I offered him some direct positive suggestions that included a feeling of self-confidence and the positive experience of speaking up and being heard to end the session. I counted backward to bring Steve back to waking consciousness.

At his next visit, Steve had experienced an enormous change. He exploded excitedly with the news that he had had a relatively difficult conversation with his two bosses. He'd persisted through it by remembering the new image of him getting what he wanted in the play area, and felt a confidence he'd never felt before.

"I wanted to stop doing the 'daily stuff' and focus on my work," he told me. "I want to work from home and have more time for myself. And now I can."

Steve looked incredibly relaxed and confident. "But I still feel like I am in a trench."

The language that my clients use (both in and out of trance) when they describe their problems is fascinating. Steve actually visualized a trench and talked a number of times about moving into a 'happy place.' Clients often refer to imaginary concrete images that appear very real to them. They believe they have a black cloud over them, or a wall or invisible shield blocking them from others. Embedded within each of these metaphors is a limiting belief. The problem is, even when my clients hear themselves saying things like, "I feel boxed in," they still don't know what to do to fix the situation.

Steve felt as though he'd been living in the trenches. But he'd never been to war. As a hypnotherapist, I'm inclined to consider the effect of past lives on a client like Steve, but I needed to go where the client was taking me. My first priority with Steve was to confront the limiting beliefs.

Ordinarily, when clients describe similarly disturbing visualizations, I try to help them overcome their limiting belief by reframing the situation. In Steve's case, I had him stand up in my office and imagine he was "in the trenches." Steve was quite apt at using his imagination to describe the dirt walls surrounding him. His imagined walls were so high that he was unable to see over them.

I asked Steve to imagine the walls slowly giving way. Slowly, he visualized the walls collapsing and the trenches filling in. As this happened, he looked around as if to be moving higher so he could look outside the trench. As Steve made his way out of the trench, his shoulders relaxed. I could see the sense of relief move through his entire body. Finally, he took a step up and out of the trench. We worked together to fill the rest of the trench in, and Steve stepped on the top of it to pound it all in. Steve was now on level ground. Then, he walked away from the trenches. He didn't have to carry this metaphor with him anymore. There was a genuine sense of amazement when we finished the vision.

Creative visualizations help clients, like Steve, to overcome the hidden, limiting beliefs and become free to experience a new perspective on life.

Steve's final visit began with an explanation of how he combined his work needs with his "me" time while he was on holiday in the UK.

Steve was happy that he was now able to be assertive with his bosses and felt a sense of power. "My wife and I went to the UK to visit with my mother. We stayed there for three weeks, and I was able to work and have plenty of time for me and my mum."

As he wanted to learn more about himself, Steve asked if we could get right to the regression, and I was happy to oblige.

As usual, we began with a relaxation meditation. As with Samantha, I guided Steve into his subconscious mind to find the part of himself that was hidden. Though the process was slightly different for Steve than it was for Samantha, the goal was still the same.

For me, the experience of guiding clients through the process of discovering hidden parts of themselves is always unique and fascinating. Every client visualizes different and unique images that serve as important clues. It is up to me to decipher these clues and then guide the client through a session that promotes healing.

During Steve's regression, he found three gray balloons. He explained that they were children's balloons. The children were at their desks, and Steven indicated to me that he had regressed to childhood. He told me that he was about six years old.

"I'm in Mrs. Smith's class," he began. "And I'm sitting next to Susan."

"Can you describe Susan to me?" I asked.

"Yes," he said and paused for a moment. "She's wearing a red cardigan, and she has long, dark hair. She put her chin on the desk. I think she's touching herself." He wanted to be friends with her, but she didn't seem interested. She didn't live nearby and had been taken away from her parents. Steve had his first crush on Susan.

He went on to explain that he felt rejected. The feelings were very fresh and powerful in his state of hypnotic trance. I continued to move him further into the regression.

"Tell me more about your experience at school," I urged him.

"There is a door to the left. It's a long school. There is a platform, stage, and a washroom. I have no friends. I have the feeling of isolation. I can see all aspects of the school." Steve

32

started to move his eyes around underneath his closed eyelids as if he were exploring and walking through the school. "There's the kitchen, the climbing frame, and the classrooms along the central hall. I am just an observer. I remember the teachers and the head mistress."

We continued the session, ending with a healing of the inner child. I guided Steve through the process of rising above the scene at the school and looking down on himself as a young child. Big Steve told little Steve all the things he knew now but wished he had known then. When he was finished with this process, I asked Big Steve to give little Steve a hug. Tears began to flow.

"I was never hugged as a child," he cried.

Emotions and feelings of isolation left this child feeling unloved and unimportant. It was at this moment that Steve had a breakthrough.

"I was never really loved," he said.

After a few more sessions with Steve, it became apparent to both of us that his time with me had ended. Steve was amazed at how assertive he had become at home and work. He even told his bosses how he felt and was very pleased with the outcome. He now has plenty of "Me time" as he can telecommute from home and when visiting his mum in Europe. And now he actually enjoys being in the office. He felt his life at home with his wife had improved so much that they planned a trip to St. Martin. As he departed my office, his final words to me were, "Life is good now."

Walled In

"The more you try to simplify things the more you complicate them. You create rules, build walls, push people away, lie to yourself and ignore true feelings. That is not simplifying things."

~ Cecelia Ahern, If You Could See Me Now

I never know which direction a hypnotherapy session will go, and I love this part of my work. This was the case with Sofia. She came to me complaining about feeling disconnected.

"I have no friends, my family is ridiculous, and I hate sex," she lamented.

She went on to explain that she had no interest in sex, and she knew her lack of interest would affect her relationship with her boyfriend.

"He's going to lose interest in me like all the other guys in my life if I can't figure out how to rev up my interest in sex."

Sofia was an intelligent and attractive 32-year-old woman, but she kept a very rigid posture in my office. I asked her about her mother.

"Mom was stupid for having given birth to me. She should have dumped my dad years ago."

Sofia's mother had two children with Sofia's father who had been a "raging alcoholic."

"Sometimes I wish I'd never been born," she said. I wondered about the strong feelings that she had toward herself and her mother. I asked her to elaborate.

"How can you stay with a man who mentally, physically, and emotionally abuses you every day?" she asked as expecting an answer from me.

Sofia admitted that the details of her childhood were ugly. She had a litany of reasons why. Her memory included a time when her father had kicked her sister in the stomach and sent her flying down a staircase. The abuse was severe and left a lasting scar. Sofia was angry with her mother for having stayed with this man who abused Sofia and her sister. It had been years since Sofia and her mother had talked.

"What about your father?" I asked." Where is he now?"

Sofia explained that after her mother finally threw her father out, he lived only blocks away yet never saw Sofia as she was growing up. At 16, Sofia went to visit her father and that meeting was the last time they spoke. Sofia felt abandoned by the people who were supposed to love her. These feelings spilled into her personal life. She had limiting beliefs about love. Her limiting belief was that people who love you will only disappoint you.

Sofia felt unworthy of love, and she lacked confidence that she would ever truly be loved.

I asked Sofia about her beliefs regarding connection and disconnection. The words eluded her. She used her hands in a pantomime gesture first and then told me, "I feel like there is a wall around me."

Similar to Steve, Sofia had created a mental wall around herself. It is very common for the mind to create images that seem so real. The wall image is one that is created to keep others at a distance to protect oneself. Sofia described the wall as though it were real because to her, it was real. A cement wall held her captive in an impenetrable fortress.

Once I had gathered a bit of information about Sofia, I felt the best technique to use would be NLP (neuro-linguistic programming). NLP is a methodology created by Richard Bandler and John Grinder in California in the 1970s. Basically, it is a science that describes how the language of the mind affects our body and behavior.

After a routine NLP induction where I guided Sophia into a quiet state of relaxation, I asked her to stand and imagine the wall that separated her from other people. I asked her to look carefully at the wall. "What is it made of?" I asked her. "What does it feel like?"

"It's large; taller than me. It surrounds me. It is made of cement bricks. It's gray and cold." I wanted her to understand how the wall was made because the next step was to destroy it.

Though Sofia had first arrived in my office as a somewhat rigid 30-something, she unabashedly smashed the imaginary wall at my bidding. She flailed her arms and her legs crushing and stomping on those cement blocks that had held her captive for so long.

When Sofia had finished demolishing the wall, I asked her how she felt.

"I feel..." she hesitated, "concerned."

"Concerned? Why?" I asked.

"I'm concerned that the wall will grow back."

Together, we decided that the best approach was to sweep up the pieces and whisk them away. Then, she got on her hands and knees and blew the leftover dust particles away.

We then began the process of returning to waking consciousness. Sofia was exhausted when she opened her eyes. That had been hard work. To her mind, the work she had just performed was "real." Sofia would sleep well that night.

A week later, Sofia returned, giddy with excitement to tell me about the progress she'd made since our previous session. She began speaking before I even had a chance to sit down.

"I have friends now," she began. "And I started doing more in the bedroom. It feels so great having nothing blocking me from people. I feel so free," Sofia explained. For the next few weeks after our first session, she pictured the fallen fortress blowing in the wind behind her. Whenever she was driving, she felt she was moving further and further away from its dust. "It's all gone now. Completely gone. And people from work were discussing where to take me to celebrate my birthday."

Sofia was beaming. The transformation was amazing.

We spoke a bit about how she was enjoying new things in the bedroom and how happy it made her and her boyfriend. They had even discussed moving in together, and she seemed more confident that the relationship had substance. Sofia was eager to learn more about herself during a regression to break through some more of her issues.

"I'm still afraid of making a fool of myself in bed. What if I do it wrong? What if I do something wrong. I'm not worthy. Not deserving. He'll disappoint me."

Sofia wanted to improve her relationship and have more intimacy with her boyfriend, so we decided to work on this issue next using regression therapy.

We began the session in the usual way. Sofia was exploring her good parts and her bad parts. I urged her to look for a "hidden" part. I could see Sofia's eyes moving beneath her closed lids.

"I'm looking at two parts, a heart and a little doll," she finally told me.

I prodded her to describe these parts.

"The heart isn't the red heart you see at Valentine's Day, but rather one with arteries and valves. The doll looks like me as a little girl. It's a little me!"

I asked her to ask the heart what it wanted from her. This is a typical question when working with parts therapy during a regression. She said the heart was tired of getting hurt. "It's to protect me from people. Hearts are soft and weak, and people make stupid decisions with the heart. It's better to use your brain."

"What does the heart want?" I asked.

"It wants love," she began, "but, it doesn't want to disappoint me. It's pushing people away. It's better without them."

"Who hurt your heart?" I asked.

"I'm so ashamed. I did something wrong. I'm not worthy. Not deserving. They disappointed me."

I turned Sofia's attention to the doll.

"It's a little me. I'm a bad person. I'm mean, I yell, I scream, I'm cold, and I push people away and make them mad."

I wanted to know more about these feelings, so I asked her to go to the first time she felt that way.

"I'm in the womb," she began. Often limiting beliefs begin right in the womb. It is actually the consciousness of the person who is well aware of everything that is happening in their lifetime at all times, even in a pre-born state.

"I don't understand. I can hear them. It's so real. There's fighting, arguing. It's very scary. Who are these people? Why are they arguing? I know I'm connected to them. I don't get it. I just want quiet. They're so annoying."

Sofia then spoke to the arguing voices, "Go away! Leave me alone! They're rude. So rude." She wasn't happy when she suddenly realized they were her parents, and she was their daughter. I was curious to know why she had chosen these bickering parents for this lifetime, and what was she to learn from them. I was surprised when she said that she was here to "teach them a lesson."

"They need to go away from each other. I want to tell them to shut up and go away. I'm getting judgmental. They're being stupid. They need some common sense."

Sofia seemed to have no understanding of her parents, especially her mother. I asked her to describe how her mother was feeling to help foster a better sense of understanding between mother and child.

"Mom is desperate. I know her story. I have no connection to her. I'm just there. She doesn't want me. She feels bad."

"Tell me about your father," I asked in an effort to encourage Sofia to better understand her father as a human being.

"He's feeling angry. She is telling him to clean up his act. He's not being a good father or husband. I agree with her. She is yelling at him. I'm cheering for her. I would have let him have it."

This was not the first time I heard that someone did not want to be a part of the family group. Sofia was definitely feeling a sense of not belonging or wanting to belong to these parents. It is interesting that these feelings were present even from the womb. I led Sofia to the moment of her birth.

"I'm not who I was supposed to be. I was supposed to be a boy. They had boys names picked out. I feel like...Haha! Gotcha! I'm just full of surprises for everybody. My father isn't there. Well, he is, but he isn't. He's too drunk. This is a mess. People are there. It just doesn't seem sincere... Wait... My Aunt is here. She seems sincere. She cares about me. I really appreciate that."

Here is a tiny newborn baby who already senses she is a huge disappointment to her family because she was not born a male. Because she was not a male, she believed she did something wrong, and now she was not worthy or deserving. Her parents disappointed her. Here it is years later, and the same thoughts are running through her mind. "What if I do something wrong. I'm not worthy. Not deserving. They disappointed me." Deep down Sofia felt that if she did something wrong, her boyfriend would disappoint her. Her heart was tired of getting hurt. And as she had just previously uttered, "Hearts are soft and weak, and people make stupid decisions with the heart."

Sofia instantly realized the connection and felt a sense of relief. Sometimes just seeing it for what it is worth allows one to break it down and whisk it away.

Baited

"When a child receives the message, even subtly or indirectly, that his emotions don't matter, he will grow up feeling, somewhere deep inside, that he himself doesn't matter."

~ Jonice Webb

Some clients struggle to open up and honestly talk about their problems. Paul was one of these clients. He anticipated not being able to explain his feelings. Before he arrived for his first session, he typed a letter to me, and when he felt comfortable with me, he pulled it out of his pocket to share. Paul was an older gentleman of 60 years or so. He was quiet and sheepish when we first met.

Sitting in the chair across from me, I noticed his zipper was unzipped. Paul explained that he was divorced. Despite being estranged from his wife, he was very close to his daughter and his son.

I unfolded the letter and read it.

Paul wanted to find out if he should remain a man or transition to a woman.

In the letter, he wrote, "If I should become a woman, would you be willing to help me by showing me how to dress, sit, act and put on make-up?"

I questioned him about his desires. He explained that for as long as he could remember, he felt he should have been born a female. He was extremely close to his mother and missed her very much. He had been her favorite child, and he enjoyed their close relationship. In his early years, he loved to fish as it was so peaceful. He used to go every weekend.

However in his later years, Paul did very little fishing. In fact, he couldn't remember the last time he went fishing. Now he spent his weekends in a much different way. Paul liked to dress in women's clothing and go to the bar on weekends. He wasn't looking to pick up anyone; he just wanted to dress up and feel like a woman. He loved watching other women and wondered how their clothing would look on him. He admitted that sometimes he would become jealous if he thought he wouldn't look as good in their outfits.

His request did not surprise me. Nor did the fact that he wanted to know more about the finer side of the female gender. As strange as the request may have seemed, I was confident that childhood or past life regression would have some answers.

Regression therapy is a very revealing process, especially when someone like Sofia regresses back to the womb. I believe that the growing fetus can understand thoughts, feelings, and words. The consciousness of the fetus is aware of what is happening inside and outside of the womb. They are aware on a soul level. They can have thoughts and feelings and create limiting beliefs right in the womb. An example of this is if a parent is concerned about the pregnancy, the unborn child can sense that. If one or both parents do not want the child, the fetus understands that too. If the parents have a gender preference, the unborn child understands that as well. Although they have no control over their gender at this stage, they are completely tuned into to the wishes, desires and thoughts of their parents.

In Paul's case, he did not regress to the womb. Instead, he regressed to the age of three or four years.

"I'm on a pier. It's the first time I've ever been fishing! I'm so excited! I'm fishing! I'm holding the pole!"

Paul described the tugging sensation on his pole and the exuberance of catching his first fish. "I turn around to show them, but nobody is there. They left me. I'm all alone holding the fish, and it is squiggling on the line."

"Why isn't anybody there, Paul?" I asked wondering myself why parents would leave a three-year-old on a pier alone.

"They went inside. They left me," his voice faltered.

"What are you thinking and feeling now?" I asked wanting to see if a limiting belief was born here.

"If I had been a girl, they would have been there. My mom would have loved me more. She wanted a girl, and I disappointed her. She doesn't love me."

Paul wasn't sure if he was alone on the pier or if someone other than his parents were there, but at the moment when he caught the fish, he felt abandoned. It was at this instant that Paul's limiting beliefs about his gender were born.

All that's necessary for a limiting belief to be born is an emotion tied to a thought. I can't emphasize this point enough, so I'll say it again. When you experience a strong emotion coupled with your thought process at a given instance based on a real experience, the two get linked together, and it can become a limiting belief in your existence.

Paul's story offers another example of how a limiting belief can be the culprit in a variety of inexplicable behaviors. Just as in Steve's case with his limiting belief about being stupid and not speaking up for oneself, Paul had a limiting belief about his gender; it would stop him from being loved.

Now these experiences are generally forgotten within a short period of time, but the limiting belief worms its way into the subconscious mind and starts fishing for validation.

The young subconscious mind (eight years and younger) lacks the ability to make reasonable judgments, so whatever goes into the subconscious mind stays there regardless of whether it is true or not. The subconscious mind is very literal. Between conception and eight years of age, these unreasonable thoughts remain unexamined. When we get older, the critical mind or sometimes our conscious mind mediates and says, "Wait a minute. That is not true." But young children believe what they are told in a very literal way. As a result, misinformation often ends up in the subconscious mind, which can cause lots of confusion later on.

Limiting beliefs that take up residency in the subconscious mind are often validated over the years, quite by accident.

These limiting beliefs are often very difficult to detect consciously. They operate in the background and wreak havoc as an annoying voice in your head. Whenever you encounter some shred of evidence that the limiting belief is a genuine and accurate portrayal of reality, you will tend to hold onto those pieces of evidence. Hypnosis allows clients to let go of the limiting beliefs and stop looking for evidence. The results are often dramatic and profoundly healing.

When Paul experienced the excitement of catching his first fish and turned around to find no one there, his disappointment and hurt along with the thought that his mother would have been there if he had been a girl, caused him to create a limiting belief. Paul wanted to be a female in order to get the attention and love that he craved. Paul healed his hurting inner child and wept as the hypnotic trance drew to a close.

"I feel tremendous relief to understand this compulsion to dress like a female," he remarked.

"Understanding the initial sensitizing events is often enough to release the belief and be able to move forward in life without the blocks," I explained.

Sometimes just the acknowledgment and understanding can help a client. A look of relief crossed Paul's face, and he left my office looking and feeling happier than when he'd first arrived.

Defiled

"...Incest is rape by extortion. Thus the child's very childhood becomes a weapon used to control her."

~ E. Sue Blume, Secret Survivors

The feeling of being physically violated is devastating, but when the abuse occurs at the hands of family members, it is even more difficult to process. The limiting beliefs that develop when a child is sexually abused are life altering.

At the age of four Loraine's older brother held her down and began a ten-year ritual of sexual assaults. At the age of nine her other brother joined in and continued raping her as well. Loraine was 52 when she came to see me. Along with the scars from being repeatedly raped during her childhood, she also had some serious anger issues. She had recently attacked a police officer, and when she first came to see me, Loraine was facing jail time, had lost her job, and was in arrears with her rent.

"Sometimes I cut myself," she revealed. "And sometimes I steal things from Walmart." She held out her arms, and I could see the remnants of her actions. Then right in front of me, as if to demonstrate her deep-rooted volatile behavior, she grabbed a pen and jabbed it into her forearm and nearly broke the skin. I quickly snatched the pen from her and looked around for any other sharp instruments that might be within her reach.

At that instant, I didn't feel I was a suitable consultant for Loraine, as her troubles seemed to extend beyond the scope of my services. "Perhaps a psychiatrist or a psychologist would be a better fit for you," I offered gently.

She explained she had already seen both as well as a counselor, but no one was able to help her.

Loraine needed help. It was obvious. She wasn't able to pay for it, but I could see in her pleading eyes that someone needed to help her. I reconsidered and offered my help.

Our first session began with the usual question and answer format to gain a better understanding of her situation. I found her story hard to believe. Actually, the word "impossible" crossed my mind. Could someone really have had such an abusive, demoralizing, and totally dysfunctional childhood filled with such a quagmire of unbelievable tales? I didn't know where to begin.

"Well, when I was four years old it was the first time when I was raped by my second oldest brother, Gary and my cousin. I vaguely remember certain things about my father, but I never fully remembered whether he raped me or not. But, I always knew something deep inside was telling me that it's possible he did. The earliest rape that I do remember is my brother Gary and my cousin at the age of four and my other brother Stan at the age of nine. And it continued until I was twenty years old. When I was ten years old, my other brother Bill entered into the picture. He learned everything from my older brother Gary. Gary taught him to take care of me, and that meant to have sex with me."

"That was taking care of you?" I wanted to know if I heard her correctly. Loraine had six older brothers. Three of her brothers had no knowledge of what was happening to their baby sister. There was Bill, who was a year older than her who in her words "did everything" to her. The abuse ranged from verbal assaults, smothering her with a pillow until she was almost unconsciousness, constantly beating her up, and sexually violating her from the ages of twelve to twenty. The next younger brother Dan physically and verbally abused her, and when she grew older, he tried prostituting her for money. Her next older brother, Mike, was hit by a car at the age of six and lived much of his youth in a body cast. He spent most of his time in and out of the hospital undergoing six different surgeries. Jerry, a year older than Mike was kind to Lorraine, although completely unaware of what was happening her. Then there was Harry.

"Yeah, that's how he took care of me until I was nine. Then Bill constantly had sex with me. And that's what he did until I was 20 years old. And at the age of--I believe it was--no, it was 17 which was the first time I told my mother, and she didn't believe me. And so I told her again. I must have been about 18 I think. And she still didn't believe me. When I was 20, Bill left marks all over my body; marks that only another person could have made. My mother finally believed me! And all she did was go straight up to him and slap him across the face. That was

51

the end of it. I was never allowed or able to talk about it. I always had to sweep everything under the rug. And that's just how my life was," Loraine expounded.

"I see," I responded trying to take it all in.

"During my elementary school years, I remember coming home from school and having to do many household chores. I never went out very much when I was a young girl I was mostly in the house. As soon as I finished school, I'd come home, prepare dinner, clean up, and then do my homework. Then it was time to go to bed. And then I worried every night whether someone was going to come into my room. I worried every night like that."

It was time to begin. I carefully guided her into her childhood memories. Each memory was more frightening than the previous. Her first memory was of her father standing naked in the living room wielding a gun at her and her mom. She was hiding behind her mother, trembling with fear. He wanted his wife to go prostitute herself for money. Loraine watched with tear filled eyes as her father physically and verbally abused her mother. This horrible abuse regularly continued until her father finally announced one day that he was leaving the family. While in her hypnotic state, I moved her along to another memory that, unfortunately, was just as traumatic. She recalled a time with her alcoholic stepfather who was also violent and abusive.

Loraine began, "He's grabbing me. Pulling me from my mom. He wants to shoot me in the head. He's crazy. He means it. The gun is at my head!"

Sadly, these horrific experiences were regular occurrences during her childhood. Finally, during a night of heavy drinking, her stepfather was waving his gun around, and then he shot himself in the head. Loraine watched in complete terror as the blood flowed, and he collapsed to the floor.

I felt it would be best to reframe her memory. As in the case of creating a polka dotted elephant, by reframing the content of a situation, the feeling of powerlessness and anger can be viewed from a different perspective. This technique empowers the individual to change their beliefs. I wanted to show Loraine how the situation that she described wasn't her fault. She could not have controlled these situations at her young age, and I also wanted to show her that having lived through these situations would give her strength. I wanted to neutralize the memories of her traumatic experiences. This technique is helpful in releasing the trauma one holds on to in cases such as rape, abuse, and combat experiences.

I had Lorraine visualize herself in a movie theater where she was watching a movie of the scenes she described. This step was necessary to detach her physically from the experience before we could remove her psychologically from the pain and terror that she was feeling. It was very difficult for Loraine to control her emotions while remembering herself in the midst of these traumatic experiences. By imagining instead that she was watching a movie of herself having the same experience, she was now able to picture it without any emotion.

Amazement came over her face when she saw just how young she was. She realized she was a victim of father and stepfather's inability to control their actions. She saw how drunk they'd become, but could not understand what that meant at the time. She realized it was their behaviors and not her behavior that was at the core of the belief, and at that tender age, she was incapable of changing anything. I had her change the movie to black and white to dissociate her from the trauma element. I then asked her to run the movie backward very quickly. This process removes ill feelings as the subconscious mind reframes the context as it blurs the event.

Loraine's shoulders relaxed as I brought her back to a complete state of consciousness. As we finished, I asked her what she learned.

"I've acted threatening when I was drinking. Now I see where that came from. I was reckless, impulsive, and irresponsible. I get it now," she uttered after she came out of the trance. "My father was a pimp. He would pimp my mother, and she would do it so that there could be food on the table for the family."

Loraine also realized that both fathers had serious anger issues and were dealing with alcoholism. She was able to recognize now that she was also an alcoholic just like her father. By gaining a better understanding of her two fathers, she was able to understand herself better. She saw that her anger towards men, in particular, mimicked what she had learned from her fathers during her childhood abuse. Loraine had been sober for nearly 11 years and the anniversary of her sobriety was approaching. She was proud of this accomplishment.

Loraine's next session focused on her six brothers. Her oldest brother, Harry, was nine years older than Loraine.

"He raped me over 200 times, I estimate. It started when I was four." She continued, "He was 13 years old when he started raping me. He told me it was my job."

We began the hypnosis session, and Loraine quickly entered a deep trance. "What are you experiencing?" I asked.

"Evil."

"Pardon?" I could not hear her.

"Evil," she spoke louder.

"What does that mean? What are you feeling?" Loraine gave no response. "Where are you right now? Describe what's around you."

"The beginning," she whispered.

"The beginning? The beginning of what?" I wanted to be sure she didn't slip into a past life.

"They are here. My brothers."

"Describe what's happening. You can float above the scene without any emotion attached to it, or you can stay in it, whichever you like. Just tell me what you're experiencing."

"It's in pain."

"Who or what is in pain?" I questioned.

"I'm in pain," she said more clearly.

"Where are you? What are you wearing?"

"Nothing. I'm in my bed. I'm not wearing anything." Loraine's face looked pained.

"You're now with them? How many are there?"

"Two, three, three!" She corrected herself.

"Who are they?"

"My two older brothers and my cousin," she described.

"And what are you afraid of?" I asked.

"They'll hurt me," she whimpered.

"Are they hurting you now?"

"Yeah," she whispered in a low, feeble voice.

"And what are they doing?"

"Hitting me with their fist and laughing at me," she began.

"And why are they hitting you?"

"I don't know." Loraine was crying like a little girl now and then became distressed.

"What is happening now?"

Loraine began thrashing her head left to right. "There's a pillow on my face. A pillow on my face! It's white. It's tight on my face." She was struggling to breathe, to be free from it.

"Is someone trying to smother you?" I asked knowing the answer already.

"So no one will hear me," she whispered.

I had her fast forward through the actual brutal raping as if watching it on a screen. I wanted to begin the process of healing her inner child by recreating her memory of this. Since the subconscious mind does not know what is real or fake, I asked her to rise above the scene to begin fabricating a new one.

"The boys are kinder now," I started. "They are gentle, and you are fully clothed and sitting on your bed. Your brothers and cousin are reading a book to you and you are enjoying the story." Loraine's face softened, but I could see she was still reeling from the images of being raped. Slowly she responded, and I could see she began enjoying creating this fanciful vision. A tiny smile brightened her face, and she put her hands under her legs and began to sway side to side like a little girl. She looked peaceful and content.

I encouraged Lorraine to imagine her older self entering the room and holding her younger self so she could share her present-day wisdom with this innocent child. Holding her arms around herself, she sobbed.

This began healing the years of abuse she had endured at the hands of her brothers. Loraine's brothers had convinced her that this is what brothers are supposed to do, and it was her job to please them. At that tender age, Loraine's critical mind was too undeveloped to process this as anything other than the truth. She connected this act of violence to mean she was loved. It was the only attention she received. In her confusion, she felt unloved by the other three brothers who did not have sex with her.

Loraine visited with me often. Each time she looked more relieved. I was glad to see the change. One day, she entered and had a huge smile on her face.

She began, "The help that you have given me is changing my life. When I substituted the thought of my brothers reading a book to me instead of raping me, it changed everything. Since I've learned that I can replace bad feelings with good thoughts as you have taught me, it just changes my whole perspective. Everything I do seems to be so much better."

"Good, I am glad to know you are able to change things for yourself and help yourself through your childhood experiences," I added.

"Yeah, you put me in another place where — like when these memories come up, I can talk about them. I feel different now 'cause I know that our God above has taken it and I know that I can put something else in its place and feel peace instead. And those two things — you and my mentor — have opened a world to me that is all brand new, all brand new."

I was glad to hear that her mentor was working with her. It is part of the fourth and fifth steps of the program where one surrenders their addiction to God.

"That's great." I was happy to see Loraine had a fresh perspective on life.

"Oh, and I have good news!" She was so excited that it made me laugh.

"I have cancer in my uterus," she announced as if she had won the lottery.

"Excuse me?" I was perplexed. "Is this the good news you are speaking about?"

"Oh, yes. I need to have a hysterectomy!" It was like she just won a million dollars.

"I'm sorry. I do not understand you. Did I miss something?" I questioned again.

She giggled like a little girl. "Don't you see?"

"Umm, no. I am afraid I don't."

"You have removed the rapes from my mind, and now God is removing the remnants from my body," she explained with her eyes beaming and a huge smile on her face.

"Oh, I see!" I responded. You learn something new every day. It was certainly a unique way of accepting such negative news about being diagnosed with uterine cancer, but I was happy that she had a positive outlook concerning it. One I never would have rationalized, yet to Loraine it was a clear revelation.

I visited her in the hospital several weeks later after her surgery, and although she was experiencing pain from the procedure, she was not permitted to have any narcotic pain relief medication. Amazingly, and by the grace of God, she was as happy as could be.

"It's all gone now," she said with a smile. "Because of you and my mentor, it's out of my mind, and now God has taken it out of my body." A look of total peace came over her. For Loraine, this was a special and wonderful gift from God.

Through the experience, Loraine and I became friends. We stay in contact, and I am happy to say that she is now living with her boyfriend and abundantly joyful. The Loraine I initially met years prior bears no resemblance to the cheerful, lighthearted woman she is today.

Concurrent Lives

"When you judge other people without wanting to know the true story behind their actions, is usually when there is something inside of you that is so broken that if you found out what you believed about them was a lie, you wouldn't want to accept it or make amends."

~ Shannon L. Alde

"Where are you?" I asked to get a better perspective on the situation she was describing.

"It's the 1800s. I am wearing Sabot, but it doesn't fit with the scene. I have on a bustled dress that's light blue. It's dark, and it looks like London. People are walking fast. It's rush hour. I'm at the corner of Baltimore Road and Mulberry Avenue. There are houses and streets only. No statues or monuments."

I waited patiently for her to continue. "I see a newspaper; it's The Arcady Post. It says it's March 5th, 1888. The headline reads: Ship Attacked. Men Dying. It's a black and white picture. Atlantic. Blaming the French."

Miriam continued and provided rich details about her location, her name, and other pertinent information.

"In my pocket there's a slip of paper. It is a Bon-Bon receipt! It's for chocolate." She laughed as she now hides chocolate under her bed so her husband won't lecture her. "I find a handkerchief with the initials MK. My name is Marianne Katz, and I'm in my 20s. I'm on my way to visit my family I think. It's dusk. I see a park. It's pretty. There are gas lamps. I'm going up the stairs of a two-story building. I don't know whose house it is. I must be rich because I am wearing an expensive dress. It's a fine dress. It's very British looking. I'm going up the steps. I am not wearing Sabots anymore. I am wearing shoes with laces that are brown."

Miriam's eyes were moving rapidly beneath her fluttering eyelids, which signaled that she was very deep in trance.

"I'm at the front door rather than the service entrance. The Servant knows me. I'm ushered into a room. It's not the living room. Is it a reception room? I don't know. A woman is greeting me. I don't think she is my mother. She is greeting me like my mother. She might be my mother. I can't tell.

"There is a little girl in the room. In this life, she is my mother. I can tell by her eyes. I'm tired. I'm going upstairs. The stairs are beautiful and have a curve. It's my bedroom, and there is a four-poster bed. It faces the park. I look out the window. Someone is in the park and is looking up at me.

"It makes me nervous. I'm scared. I closed the window. I locked it and moved back from it. I'm changing clothes for dinner. I have to dress formally. My little sister or mother comes in. Her hair is in curls. She's a brat. I love her, but she is a brat. I hear the dinner bell.

"We must have a lot of money. The cook, butler, server and I don't have to wash the dishes! Ha! We are waiting for the main course. This is my sister's house. The girl is my niece. I've been taken in. Her husband comes in. I don't like him. He makes me nervous too. I guess I have no choice. I don't know what happened to my parents, but they are no longer there. My sister's husband doesn't want me there. He is tolerating me. He doesn't like me. The women are going into the reception room and doing handiwork, embroidery, and heirloom work. (Laughing) Smocking. I do that now. Smocking is embroidering pleats in dresses. My niece is learning to work with a needle."

Suddenly, Miriam's demeanor changed.

"Something is happening. The front door slams. My brother-in-law is yelling at a man. My sister and I don't want to find out. He is going to be nasty and angry. He tells me to come out. He introduces me to an old man. The man is about 50 years old. He says I am going to marry him. I run out and up to my bedroom. The same person was looking at me from the park. I am crying on my bed. Like hell I am going to marry him! My sister and brother-in-law are yelling. I don't like that. He will slap her. He's done it before. I would never let anybody hurt her . . . Oh, the little girl is not my niece! She's mine. No wonder he didn't want her here. It's getting dark. I'm coming back. I'm crying and hugging Stella, my daughter . . . It's another day, and my daughter and I are going somewhere. I have a bag with me and a suitcase. I'm crying. I think my brother-in-law has thrown us out. I'm just walking. I see that man across the street. I can't see any more. I'm holding Stella's hand . . . Now, I'm at my wedding. I'm not marrying the old man; I'm marrying a young man. He's my daughter's father. She looks just like him. She is very happy. My sister is also there, but my bother-in-law is not. The old man is there. He's standing up. This is his son . . . We are in the country somewhere. I'm riding in a coach with horse. I am old now. I cross over, and my husband is there. My husband. Reconnection. I was damn lucky in that lifetime. If he hadn't married me, I don't know what I would have done. We are running in the fields, both young again. Just like the last time I saw him. He died in WWI. We are happy to be reunited. It's like we were never apart. So much love here. Amazing!" Miriam was beaming now.

The nice part about being a hypnotist is showing people that we all come around together over and over. If you were the father in one lifetime, you might be the daughter in the next. A rich, exciting life can be followed by a poor devastating one. Anything is possible. But what I didn't expect to happen, happened in her next session with me.

Miriam popped into another lifetime almost before I could say, "Sleep!" It has been proven that one goes deeper and deeper after each hypnotic experience. In fact, it is a deepening technique to put someone into a trance, then take them out and put them back in again. This was not necessary with Miriam.

She went under rapidly. "I'm alone. It's dark here. I'm alone and it's dark. I see the moon over the water. Things are beginning to take shape. I have no shoes on. I am wearing a long dress. Victorian type with the waist pinched in. I see a light in the distance. I'm walking toward the light." I move her forward in this past lifetime.

"I'm watching a debutante party. It's in a big hall and it's very bright and light. I'm not in the hall, but standing back in the distance watching. It's definitely at least 150 years ago. I don't like these people. They're very snobby. I'm not going out on the dance floor like I am supposed to. Several girls are taking me and pushing me out on the dance floor. I'm dancing almost like I'm in a Balzac novel. I'm running out to the garden. There's a young man there. I hide. I don't belong here. I want to go home." Miriam felt uncomfortable in this opulent environment. I suggested she move to the next significant time in that life.

"I'm in NY, I think, but I can't be. I'm on the street watching people dying. It's the Triangle Shirt Factory fire. People are dying; jumping out of windows. It's gruesome. Awful. I'm walking away. I can't stand it. I'm going home. I'm walking up the stairs in an apartment building. I don't belong here either. I think I'm renting or a boarder. It's not my family." Then she moves forward in time without my prompting her.

"I'm working — it's Pittsburg of all places. The irony of it all," she says as she's laughing. "I'm a house maid. Oh boy did I come from the wrong place," she laughed. "I'm taking care of a house and children. Not mine. Strange that I would be taking care of a house," laughing now even harder. "I hate to cook. I hate to clean. It's funny that I am taking care of this house and I don't do a thing in mine." She was referring to her life today. Apparently she had enough cleaning in her last lifetime so she doesn't like to clean her house in this one.

Miriam continued, "I'm getting old. Dying. The lady of the house and the doctor are there. I'm dying." I was about to ask her the usual questions I would typically ask at this time about life, lessons, but she beat me to it. "I don't know what was learned. Recipes I guess," laughing again. "It was a good family.

My daughter is one of the children I took care of. She came back as my daughter in this lifetime." Miriam knew the drill by this time and now she summarizes her own past life regressions. "I'm on the beach again," she continued as she popped into another life. "I'm with my two little boys. They're mine. Digging sand castles. We are on Coney Island. That's home for my grandsons and me. It's before WWI. I'm in a bathing suit Fluffy legs — so funny looking." Here, Miriam is with her two boys, who are her two grandsons in this lifetime.

She mind-travels again.

"It's not good," she began. "It's the flu. I'm very sick. I'm not dying yet but very sick. I'm having trouble breathing. It's not the flu. It's TB." At this point in our sessions, the client knows to keep expressing what is happening so I don't interrupt the vision. "I see myself in a crematorium. My grandfather is there. I've passed away and . . . so has he.

"I see my mother. She is a little girl. She was Grandfather's little girl. He died when she was very young. That must have been terrible for her."

Then she continued, "I'm leaving," and before I could speak, she continued, "I'm a little girl." Confused by this statement, I asked her to explain. I wanted her to review the last lifetime she'd described, to tell me the lessons that she gained from her experiences, but instead of reviewing her life, she moved right into another one.

"I'm in an orphanage. I live there. I'm wearing a pink dress with a tunic. It's not very clean. Nor am I! Oh, look! There's Miri!"

Often clients recognize people from their current lifetime as someone they knew in the past. This piqued my interest.

"Who is Miri?" I asked.

"It's me. I'm Miri." She told me. "I'm watching me. I'm watching everything that is happening to me."

"So you are a little girl in an orphanage looking at yourself when you were a little girl in the orphanage in this lifetime?"

"Yes." I furrowed my brow when she said this. It didn't make sense.

"I hear Miri yelling to her daddy. She's telling him not to leave her there. He's so mean. Just so mean." Then Miriam spoke, "I don't want to see this. What he did to my brother and me."

As the session continued, I learned that in the late 1960s and early 1970s, when Miriam had been a little girl in this lifetime, she and her brother had had a horrific experience. Early in this lifetime, her mother became very ill. Her father decided he could not take care of his sick wife and the two little children. So Miriam and her brother (who had a mental illness) had to go. Lying to everyone including his wife, Miriam's father explained to his wife that the children would be staying with family members. But instead he took his son to Willowbrook; a place renowned as terrifying and unethical where over 6,000 mentally disturbed children lived in filth and dirt. Then he took Miriam to an orphanage. She pleaded with him not to leave her there, but he was unresponsive. Years later, Miriam's aunt had found out about the children and rescued Miriam. Miriam, now much older, went and found her brother and moved him out of Willowbrook.

Miriam was reliving her terror from another child's point of view; watching herself be dropped off in this life at the orphanage and abandoned as she begged and pleaded with her father not to leave her there.

"It was awful," she started as she awakened from a deep trance. "It was so mean of my father to do that to us."

I wasn't sure what to say. I had never experienced anyone revisiting their current lifetime through a past life regression.

I had studied "Concurrent Lifetimes" in my courses for regression therapy, but until I had this session with Miriam, it didn't resonate with me. The first lesson that I learned about concurrent lifetimes is that all time exists now. We tend to imagine time as a series of sequential events that could be placed along a continuum that moves from the past to the present to the future. While I was learning about concurrent lifetimes, I watched a demonstration about how people visualize time differently. A group of people was asked to close their eyes and to point one finger to the past and with the other hand point one finger to the future. Each person pointed to a different place. One person pointed to the sky for the future, and behind for the past. Another person pointed to the front of the room for the future and the back of the room for the past. While still another pointed left for the future and right for the past. People view time differently. Everyone tends to hold a unique image as to where the past, present, and future are located. But what if the past, present, and future existed all at once? Where would you point to then? Imagine all of your lifetimes past, present, and future existing at the same time. This is a difficult concept to understand and when first hearing it, I thought it was impossible. Where was the proof? I was open to the idea of reincarnation so the idea of lifetimes happening simultaneously shouldn't be too far of a stretch for me either, but I still struggled with it. Miriam's session helped me to understand the idea of concurrent lifetimes better though. Parallel universes and concurrent lifetimes are all happening at this very moment whether we are aware of them or not. In this lifetime, you could be having another experience as the opposite gender, in a different country, or with different parents or even in a different era.

Miriam was excited when she arrived for her next session a week later.

"I had an epiphany last week," she began to explain. "I realize that I don't cry. I didn't even cry when I lost my twins."

Miriam's first pregnancy was unplanned and she'd had a miscarriage in her first trimester. A few years later, after she married and settled down, she became pregnant again and was excited to be having twins: two boys. At the beginning of the eighth month she went into labor. The first baby was still born and the other survived for only 36 hours. She lost them both and didn't shed a tear.

"I learned early in life that showing emotion made you look weak. So I didn't cry as a child, and I haven't cried since." After the twins, Miriam and her husband went on to have another, healthy child named David. Miriam then had another miscarriage.

"And I never cried about it, which was very strange."

Miriam and her husband eventually had two additional girls, two years apart, Leah and Naomi.

"In my head, I named the boys Abdul and Mohammad, two names I would have never considered." She explained that she felt angry all the time.

"I've tried to talk to my husband, but he doesn't seem to understand," she told me. "I feel like this lifetime is a useless journey."

We began that hypnotic session to try to better understand Miriam's anger and her feeling that this lifetime had no purpose. Miriam was able to go into a deep trance quickly and hypnotic suggestions easily became her reality. Following my lead, she went to a beautiful garden, a peaceful and forgiving garden with beautiful fountains and a wooden bridge over a stream of water. On one side of the bridge, the water was choppy and rough, but on the other side the water was calm and serene. When she walked over the bridge, she found a new path where she could go to leave the past behind and find a release from the burden she was carrying with her.

"There's a reason to continue on this path because there's knowledge to be learned along the way," I explained.

"I see images," she began and I knew we were on the right track. "I don't want to see them."

"Who's with you?" I asked.

"My father. And my mother. I don't want to see either of them."

"They have a message for you," I suggested. "They have something to tell you that you've been longing to hear."

"My mother is holding the hands of two children," she explained. "They are my children. My boys. Oh . . . they're my boys." Her face brightened.

I hoped that Miriam would get some closure through this hypnotic encounter with her parents and the boys she lost.

"My father is telling me he was afraid, but I don't know what he was afraid of. He won't tell me. He is standing there looking at me as though he is weak and forlorn, but I don't care. I don't want to forgive him. How do I forgive someone who has hurt me so badly?"

Miriam needed some time before she would be able to forgive her father. This is the first time she'd seen him in spirit. When her brother had passed over and he was interred in a grave near those of her parents, Miriam had purposely kept her back to her father's headstone.

"Grandma is here and Grandpa too," she continued. "My Bother is here. He seems to have forgiven my parents for all those years of torment."

I waited.

"But, I'm not willing to forgive."

I decided to concentrate on her mother and her two children. "Talk to your mother."

"She says she's sorry. She didn't mean to hurt me. She is saying that she loves me and hopes I will forgive her . . . but I won't. Her words leave me feeling cold. Words don't mean anything. I'm not ready to forgive." This was understandable given the pain that Miriam had experienced throughout her life because of her parents' inability to care for her and her brother. I had hoped to come back to this issue at a later time.

"She is pushing the boys to me. I'm shocked that she would do that. They want me to love them. How can I love someone I've never held?" She wondered this out loud, and I wondered what she meant. I learned later that one child was stillborn and even though the other boy lived for 36 hours, Miriam had not been allowed to see the son who survived. I wanted her to feel the love from these two baby boys that she'd missed so I asked her if she would be willing to hug the boys.

"They're hugging me now," she reported, and a smile came to her face and her expression changed. She took a deep breath. "I can love them now. I can feel their love and it's intense." She smiled again gently.

"Ask your boys why they didn't survive?" I asked hoping that insight would help Miriam experience a sense of closure.

"They said it wasn't their time."

She paused and took a breath. "But why did I have to go through that?" No answer came to her.

"The scene is changing. My mother, my cousin and the boys are in NY where we used to go for the summer. I am my cousin now and it's as if they are 'her' boys. It's like we switched places. I'm not there anymore. It's my mother, Barbara and the boys. Their names are Mark and Anthony. They didn't like the Arabic names Abdul and Mohammad. Ha!" She laughed. "They're five years old now and Barbara is there as me. That's what makes my mother happy. The family is all there. All of my father's cousins are there."

"Why are you being shown this scene?" I asked, as I was confused.

"Because I love the family and I can feel their love."

I was relieved that Miriam was able to see that the family was warm and loving in another place and time. I let her relive this warmth for a while.

"Are you ready to forgive your mother now?" I asked her.

"I think so."

"What is happening now?" I questioned.

"She wants to give me a hug."

"Will you let her?" I offered.

"I guess so." I watched as Miriam moved around in the chair as if to make it easier for her mother to reach around her. Suddenly, tears emerged and started flowing from her eyes. I asked her to hug her mother like they had never hugged before.

Then came a quiet whisper. "I love you, Mom." And the session ended.

Falling Into Worthlessness

"No one can declare your feelings and emotions illegal or judge them unworthy. You feel what you feel."

~ Charles F. Glassman, Brain Drain The Breakthrough That Will Change Your Life

Clients who are fighting with the scale and losing the battle often come to see me complaining that they don't understand why they can't lose a few pounds.

"I'm eating healthy, not drinking, exercising every day, and I still weigh the same."

When I hear these words, I always wonder what is burdening them. What in their life is weighing them down? Is it a memory, an old limiting belief, a fear or a protective shield?

When Jon came to me, he wanted to lose 100 pounds. He was quite overweight and told me how his weight had held him back from being happy.

Jon fell easily into a trance, and we began work that had to do with inspiring Jon to feel motivated to exercise and control his portions. After we had completed this part of the session, I asked Jon to find the part of himself that was hidden; the part that John wanted to protect and cover-up.

"It's orange and it fits in the closet," he told me. "It has been in the closet for a long time. It has to do with courage."

"Tell me more, Jon." I encouraged him.

"It has wanted to come out and be wanted. It has learned that it's O.K. to make mistakes."

Suddenly, Jon's facial expression changed and he began describing a scene at a construction site with his dad when he was five years old. They were looking for a new home.

"I wasn't paying attention. I backed up and fell out of a window, and my dad freaked out. He was terrified."

This must have been a traumatic experience for a young child to live through, so I wanted to know more concerning his beliefs about it. I asked Jon to continue.

"I broke my collar bone. I ruined it for everybody," he explained. "I felt like I ruined everyone's day. When I was in the hospital, I felt like it was taking too much time. Like I was a burden." Jon's consideration for ruining everyone's day was more important than breaking his clavicle. He felt unworthy of the time spent in the hospital and believed that his family would rather have been doing something else.

When a person feels unworthy, they may actually create a real-life situation for themselves so they can experience it more profoundly in an effort to master it. From that point forward, Jon continued gaining weight, which limited the opportunities he had to feel worthy.

Once a limiting belief is stored in the subconscious mind, it constantly looks for validation. When validation is found, it says, "See, I told you so, you are unworthy!"

The weight kept Jon feeling "unlovable" which in turn made him feel "unworthy" of love. So to validate the belief, Jon kept eating. He wore his weight like a coat of protection and wearing this coat allowed him to continue to feel unworthy. Once Jon realized this, he began to understand his weight better. The protective shield that it seemingly provided was no longer necessary.

Withholding Love

*Shame, blame, disrespect, betrayal, and the
withholding of affection damage the roots from which
love grows. Love can only survive these injuries if they
are acknowledged, healed and rare."*

~ Brené Brown, The Gifts of Imperfection

A beautiful woman bounced into my office, observably excited
to have a hypnotic session. She was a flight attendant with an
abundance of high energy and personality. I liked her
immediately. Sandra explained that she initially wanted to see
me for smoking cessation, but due to scheduling difficulties,
sufficient time had elapsed for her to quit the habit on her own.

She reassured me that she was completely over the smoking habit. Instead, she wanted to work on relationship issues. Sandra, as she put it, always seemed to pick the same man in a different suit.

"The men I date are always emotionally unavailable," she told me.

We discussed this problem in greater depth and then I asked about her father.

"I don't speak with my dad. He doesn't like me. But I do see my mom."

I began by explaining that very often clients will come to see me with a specific issue to work on. However, the subconscious mind has such a different thought process that invariably what one consciously perceives to be the problem turns into something entirely different.

"You never know where a hypnotic trance will lead you and I have to work with what shows up for you," I explained.

We decided to see where Sandra's subconscious mind would lead us. I spoke gently while guiding her into a deep state of relaxation until I saw the flutter of her eyelids, and I knew she had entered a trance state.

We began by looking for a hidden part. Sandra had difficulty finding hers. "I feel something, but it is not a part. I feel like it is a memory."

"Your memory is a part of you," I explained delicately. "Let's find out more about this feeling," I urged.

"The memory has turned into a word now," she whispered as she furrowed her eyebrows.

"What is the word?" I asked.

"CHILDHOOD," she said. "The word CHILDHOOD in big, giant letters like a huge sign. It fills up the whole room. It's dark blue."

At that point, I guided Sandra away from parts therapy and into a childhood regression.

"It feels lonely and abandoned. I'm a baby, and I'm sitting upstairs in the living room. I'm upstairs in our house in my grandmother's apartment. She lives up there. It's safe here. I feel safe. I can smell my grandmother. She is warm. I'm here because my father is keeping my mother from me."

Then Sandra broke into laughter, "This is so friggin' cool! I can see I'm wearing a crocheted jumper. My mother made it for me. She loved to crochet, and she was good at it. I can see the jumper. It is off white with little pink flowers on it. I am loving this!"

"Why are you separated from your parents?" I asked her gently to investigate her earlier comment.

"Father is keeping me from my mother," she repeated.

"Sandra, can you tell me what your father is feeling and why he is keeping you away from your mother?"

"Jealousy. Rage. Not wanting to share. He doesn't want to share my mother with me. It's control. He's jealous. His mother was emotionally unavailable to him, and he is jealous that mother is giving me attention. I think he thought that he would always get attention from her, and he is short-changed again."

As I wondered what limiting beliefs Sandra had developed during this time, she must have been wondering the same thing. She asked out loud, "Why would you feel like withholding love? There is enough love for everybody so give it to me, the baby."

I wasn't surprised by her question. Even a three week old knows there is enough love to go around. I asked her what lesson she needed to learn from the experience.

"I shielded myself. As a baby, I shielded myself so I wouldn't be happy again. Oh, look, the word has changed. It is no longer big anymore. It's tiny and little and pink! Oh, it's jumping around and skipping, it's free now."

Sandra realized through this regression why she was choosing men who were emotionally unavailable. It was her protective shield. Now, her choices in men could change as she became emotionally available and open to finding the same in a lover.

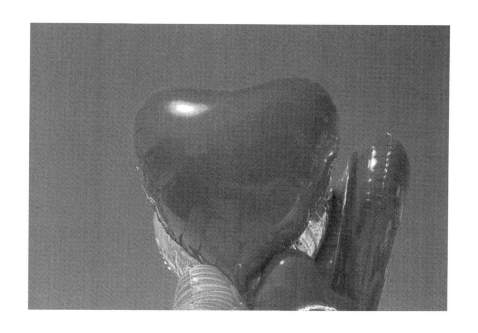

Fun Equals Pain

"But if there is an absence of such validation of a child's importance to the parent, if a child is made to feel shame for wanting or needing attention often enough, she will grow up being blind to many of her own emotional needs."

~ Jonice Webb, Running on Empty: Overcome Your Childhood Emotional Neglect

Jennifer loved to dance. She called me wanting to know if I could help her get over her fear of dancing in public. However, when she arrived, she had given it more thought and asked if we could work on social anxiety instead.

"I think my fears go deeper than just dancing. I want to feel more comfortable in social situations and business meetings."

Jennifer was a finance director, and she spent more time in meetings than she wanted. Her nervousness in social situations started when she was 18 years old. She had moved to a small high school where everyone had known each other since they were in kindergarten.

I asked Jennifer about dancing.

"I guess I'm just afraid of looking silly. Whenever my dad would watch TV, he would see other women dancing and moving their bodies. He'd say they looked trashy. Dancing was bad. It was immoral."

"Tell me more about your dad." I encouraged her.

"Oh, I don't know..." she hesitated. "He never really showed any emotion."

It took some time for Jennifer relax sufficiently to enter a trance state, but when she finally entered, I asked her to begin looking for the part of her that she was covering up. She opened the closet door.

"It's a heart shaped balloon . . . a red one. It smells like citrus, and it's the size of a basketball. It's hiding because it's scared. If it comes out, something will hurt it."

Hearts always get broken, but I wanted to know about the first time Jennifer's heart was broken.

"I'm in our apartment. I'm about four years old or younger. I am excited. I tried to talk to my father, but I can't pronounce the words properly. Kaka, I say K's instead of T's. He gets really mad at me and tells me if I can't pronounce it properly not to talk to him anymore until I could say the word right. I'm so sad now. I was so happy and wanted to tell him something, and now I just feel I'm unlovable. I guess I'm not worthy of his time if I can't speak right."

I needed to know what her belief was about this. She wasn't sure at first. I sat patiently with her until the words to describe the limiting belief came to her.

"Unless I can do something perfectly, I'm not worth their time."

"What do you think you learned from this experience in your life?" I asked.

"That it's not true. I am worthy."

Even at the young age of four, children have a very keen understand of what is going on around them. They understand how people are feeling, what they are thinking, and why they are doing what they may be doing. They're not sufficiently able to communicate their thoughts, but they understand much more than they generally get credit for. They perceive their world by someone's tone of voice, their actions, their words, and even their movement. They understand everything.

I asked Jennifer what her father was feeling and why he was so hard on her.

Jennifer hesitated before responding. Her eyes were closed and her brow furrowed. Finally, she answered, "He was worried I would never talk properly, and he would be embarrassed."

Finally, I asked her to hug her inner child and tell her inner child all the things she knows now and wishes she had known then. When she gave the signal that she was finished talking to her inner child, we moved on.

"Ask the heart if it is ready to come out now."

"No. The heart is still scared."

"Where does it want to go now?" I asked.

"I came home from visiting an aunt down the street. I was having a really good time. When I got home, I got a whipping with a belt because I wasn't supposed to be at my Aunt's house. I was in shock. I didn't expect to get in trouble for going there. I got confused that sometimes things will turn out bad even if I don't understand why."

I asked her to describe what she believed to be true at that time.

"If I do what I want to do – something fun – I might get in trouble for it."

"The lesson learned is that it wasn't fair what happened to me, and my fears shouldn't stop me from enjoying life. The heart now changed from red to an orangish-yellow, and it is much smaller, lighter, and happier."

Here is a woman whose limiting beliefs have stifled her from enjoying life. She was afraid to dance because she felt people would think she looked silly. She was uneasy in a public speaking situation because she lacked the confidence that she could speak properly. As a child, she was conditioned to feel that she should not speak because of her father's embarrassment. Even though Jennifer's mother worked with her to pronounce her words, her father made her feel insignificant. Her association with having fun or a good time was that she may be doing something wrong and get seriously reprimanded for it. Having fun at her aunt's house got her a beating by her father with his belt.

According to Anthony Robbins, there are six human needs: certainty, variety, love/connection, growth, contribution, and significance. Jennifer's father not only took a sense of significance from Jennifer, but he also challenged her certainty. This confused Jennifer. Since her critical mind was not developed by that age, her limiting beliefs became: if I have fun and enjoy myself, I may get a beating.

This limiting belief created an inner conflict, and Jennifer questioned whether she should have fun. Will I get in trouble for it? She wondered. Who can enjoy life with the threat of negative consequences weighing on every decision one makes? These thoughts were hidden deep in Jennifer's subconscious mind and needed to be reframed.

Jennifer's inability to speak properly at age four now influences how she feels when she has to speak in front of a group of people. If her own father didn't want her to talk to him, then how could she feel comfortable talking to her colleagues? This inner conflict needed to be reframed. Once Jennifer realized where her feelings of fear initially came from, she was able to begin to heal her inner child.

Jennifer and I re-created the scene with her father. She was once again excited and wanted to share it with her father. This time, her father ignored her inaccurate pronunciation, grabbed her, swung her around and kissed her on her forehead. This new image will create the foundation for a new belief that she will not be humiliated when she speaks publicly.

Before the age of eight, children will believe what they hear, what they are told, and the thoughts they have as a result. Right or wrong, true or false, their subconscious mind remembers it all and is always looking for validation.

I Hate My Mother!

"You may shoot me with your words, you may cut me with your eyes, you may kill me with your hatefulness, but still, like air, I'll rise!"

~ Maya Angelou

The Akashic Records, which is also known as "The Book of Life," have become a very important part of my work with clients. The term Akasha was introduced into the language of theosophy in the 1800's and has had a profound impact on spiritual studies thanks to individuals like Edgar Cayce. For the sake of brevity and simplicity, one way to understand the Akashic Records is to think of them as a book titled, The History of Your Soul. It is an energetic imprint (or book) that contains the entire history of your soul including every thought, action, emotion, and experience that has ever occurred to you in time and space. It contains all past, present, and future possibilities through the vibrations of love, compassion, and joy. It is like the DNA of the universe. 'Akasha,' a Sanskrit word meaning sky, space or aether, contains all knowledge of human experience written into the fabric of all existence. The records or The Book of Life exist on a nonphysical plane and further described as a library that can be accessed through the superconscious mind while in a deep hypnotic trance.

A woman named Laurie called me one morning in a panic. "I can't stand it anymore. I need to know why I was born to these horrible people!" Fortunately for her, someone had rescheduled their appointment that day, and I was able to fit her into my schedule.

"I hate my mother. In fact, I hate my entire life. My girlfriend even said to me that I have a shitty life." Laurie was adamant.

I figured she must have just had an argument with her mother given her impassioned commentary. But I was wrong. Very wrong. Both her parents were deceased; her mother had passed nearly 15 years ago. I wondered why she was so fervently venting. I wanted to know more about their relationship and the patterns in her life that made her feel this way.

She continued, "People steal from me. My entire inheritance was stolen from me. I have had six deaths, I fell and injured my hip, I was fired from my job, and a dog mauled my face."

I could certainly see why she felt the way she did, and before I could say anything, she continued her rant.

"I was yanked out by forceps, my mother hit me every day of my life, I was molested by a neighbor between the ages of five and nine. I have the highest IQ, and I skipped kindergarten." She spoke as though her world was about to end.

Laurie was also unhappy with her weight. She believed that she was holding onto her weight for protection. I agreed with her and explained that many victims of abuse have a tendency to remain overweight almost as if to say to the world, "Look, I'm not attractive. You don't want me. Go find someone else to abuse."

We had a lot of work to do. I was sure a childhood regression would reveal answers, but we would have to go deeper. We began the hypnosis part of the session, and she easily went into a state of deep relaxation. She immediately recalled one happy memory.

"Wow, I really had a happy moment with my mom!" She seemed amazed. "We are in the children's section of the library. I am four years old and read all of the books in this section. The librarian is impressed. My mother is beaming as if she held the prize. That is all I am to her. A thing. Some 'thing' she can own."

I wanted to move on, but Laurie wanted to stay in that moment. I explained she could take this memory with her, and that was enough to encourage her to move along.

Her next memory did not turn out as happy. It was at her bas mitzvah. "I am so excited to finally read from the Torah and celebrate this day. I am so proud of myself. I am at the podium, and I'm reading. Everyone is looking at me. I'm doing an excellent job." A few quiet moments passed as she was obviously enjoying this second memory. "I'm in the parking lot now. I'm in the car with my mother. She's hitting me. She's hitting me because she was not happy with my reading. I embarrassed her. She keeps hitting me. Why was I born to this miserable person?"

At Laurie's next session, she collapsed in my chair and announced that she wanted to understand why she always felt that she was on the outside looking in. "Why did I choose these people and such a difficult life?" She asked. We decided to continue with regression therapy in search of the answer to that question. In vitro, a fetus understands what is happening inside and outside the womb. As strange as it may sound, what's revealed from a person's time in the womb can be cathartic.

When Laurie reached her trance state under hypnosis, she began her regression by stating, "I am caught between wanting to go in utero or ... Or ... I feel sheer terror. It's nice ... Floating ... If I only focus on the physical, then I feel safe. The water feels nice. When my mind goes outside, I feel rage, anxiety and terror. I see red. She (her mother) is red. Her anger is like flames I don't want to touch or leave my little space. I look at her with fear. I look outside, and I peer through the walls. I see fine. I feel terror in my chest, straight to my throat. I'm terrified of leaving where I am. It's not safe outside. Her rage touches me."

"What is your mother thinking, feeling?" I asked.

"She hates me. She hates everyone. She is telling someone, 'I hate you!'"

I wanted her to understand more from her mother's point of view. "How does she feel about being pregnant?" I asked. I wondered if perhaps her mother had not wanted the pregnancy.

"She's conquered something. She feels entitlement, and she sees ownership. I'm a 'this' not a person, not a baby. What I am is a conquest. She might be feeling it towards her sister. She is better because she owns what's inside. She feels like 'This is mine!' when she thinks about being pregnant with me. I don't feel she has any pride or happiness about being pregnant. There is a major disconnect here. Not a bonding. Not a love. No love. It's a cerebral/childlike selfishness. I could be a crayon. I'm not a baby to her. Wow — I feel absolutely no love for me growing inside of her. I'm an 'It.' For her, it's a 'get back' at my father. She is showing everybody that she's going to own something, and she's going to take me away — away from my father." Laurie continued detailing every second of her experience. She continued without prompting; "Now she's telling my father, 'I am going to have her. She is going to be mine and no one else will have her.' Wow, no feeling for me. No connection. I'm just a possession. It's flipping me out. It's scary to come out. She hates me. She doesn't want to do anything for me."

It was time to be born. "NO! I won't go! I don't want to be born. I'm holding on!" Lauric's arms were now above her head like she was holding on to a life raft to save herself. "I'm two weeks late. They are pulling me out. I feel the cold forceps pulling at me." Laurie wasn't happy about being born.

I changed the direction of her trance and asked her to float back to a time before she entered the womb. I wanted to explore the time before her decision to be born again (reincarnated), the time she spent in a spiritual state between lives.

She went there almost immediately. "I don't want to leave here. It's such a pretty place, but I have anxiety because I am going back. I am standing, but there is no ground beneath me.

I am child size. I have the body of a seven-year-old, but my mind is an adult's. I am aware of other beings, other souls — except God. I hear a voice say, 'You have to pick somebody. You need to learn to love.'"

I waited while Laurie tried to understand why she chose her mother and father as parents.

"I picked my mother because she is the least lovable and . . . wow, but she is so aloof. If I can love her enough, I can help her. If I love her enough, I could fix that part of her. She is cold. This bitch is cold. I feel impatience around me."

"What is the process you need to go through?" I asked Laurie. I wanted to help her understand the steps she could take to find love for such a cold woman.

"I see her, and I see my father. There's a row of people in the background. It's like I'm watching a play. Two people step into the light while the rest are in the shadows. I choose my father by default. I feel anxiety. I don't feel loved. I felt nothing before I selected them. He was my child, but I don't feel love for him. It feels natural that he is coming with me. My mother scares me. I don't know who she was to me. I see my grandmother. I have a major connection with my grandmother. It seems like my grandmother and I were one at one time. This woman who is to be my mother is growing larger. She's big. Her presence is huge. My father's presence is much smaller. He is just there. I feel like I'm his mother, and I feel I need to teach him something. Too bad I wasn't my mother's mother. She is miserable. Why the fuck did I pick this woman? She is unyielding like a statue. It feels like she's thinking, I dare you to pick me.'"

Laurie went on to describe the other people around her. "I feel my grandmother's gentleness. There is nobody else to pick, but maybe I can heal her? She's broken. She doesn't even smile when I pick her. I just heard my mind say, 'She hates you,' but it's more complicated than that. My grandmother said she doesn't hate me, but rather that she's jealous of me. I feel terror. I don't see anyone else to choose from. I have to take my mother to teach her, and she's not grateful. She's really void of any feeling, happiness, or want. I feel like I don't have a choice about it. I keep hearing if I love her, I can heal her. My father is just coming along for the ride. He's not as spiritually developed as she is. The light is shining on her, and I'm stuck with her. She's the only one to pick. I'm doing this lifetime for her. It's not about me. Spiritually, I'm much older than she is, and I am choosing her as a parent but I feel like I'm the parent. Why are these my only choices?" Laurie asked in desperation.

When she came out of the regression, Laurie was amazed. She was astonished at how her mother had had absolutely no feelings or love for her. Her mother's apathy was immense. Laurie was still fixated on why she had no other mother figure to choose from. I explained that we live many lifetimes. Sometimes we're the mothers, sometimes we're the daughters, sometimes we're rich and other times we're poor. Perhaps there was a balancing of energy that needed to occur, or karma that had to be reconciled through Laurie's mother-daughter relationship.

Laurie scheduled another session for a week later. At her next session, I suggested to Laurie that her answers may be found in her Akashic records.

After a brief discussion concerning the Akashic Records, I guided Laurie to the Hall of Records to possibly find answers to the problems stemming from her relationship with her mother. Laurie's eagerness accelerated the hypnotic induction, and Laurie found herself in the record's library almost immediately.

"It's huge! I mean, it's unending!" she corrected herself. "There are no walls or floor to it. It's a giant library. There doesn't seem to be an end to it. The shelves are very dark wood and filled with books, but the books aren't sitting on the shelves, they are sort of floating in their space."

I could see her eyes darting about under her lids. She was searching, scanning, scrutinizing, and inspecting every inch of this awesome place. Then someone appeared to her.

"It's my guide. Oh, good, he is going to show me something. I am to follow him, but I don't know how I know that. But I just know I need to follow him."

I asked if she had a form, a shape, a body — not wanting to be too specific, but she couldn't see herself. "I know I have a body though — I just can't see it." However, Laurie was able to see her guides form, and she described it to me. "He's old. He has very white hair and a long white beard. He's wearing a white robe. He looks like a wizard. He has little wings on his back, but he's not using them to move forward. I don't see any feet either; he is just sort of floating forward. Everything is very high up. I just keep looking up, and it is an endless array of shelves with books. He brings me to my book. It has a white cover; it doesn't look like it can fit on a shelf. It's the size of an unabridged dictionary. The cover is fluffy like one of those fancy photo albums, and it has no writing on it, no name or anything."

"How do you know that this is your book?" I asked her.

"It lit up for me. It's the only one that lit up. Only my white book and my guide are glowing."

I let her get a good look at her book.

"Normally, I don't like being in crowded places. When I'm around a lot of people, my chest feels heavy — but now that I have my book, I feel better."

"Is it time to open the book?" I asked.

"It looks heavy, too heavy to hold since I am floating. She smiled. "It's too heavy to hold."

"Do you need your guide to help you open the book?" I wondered.

"The book is a secret. I feel possessive of it as well. I need a desk. Oh, I'll just have one float up to me. Wow, that's neat. The pages are all white. There's nothing on them, blank. Hmmm . . . When I open it up, the left side has square corners, but the right side of the book has curved corners. The corners are embellished. I hear the words, 'The information is conveyed to you.' I hope this isn't in Hebrew," she giggled. "I see some letters now, written in with thick ink. The letters are old fashioned like they were written with quill ink. The man with the white beard is still here. He's just hanging around." She giggled again. "So when I look into the book, I can't read the darn thing."

"Perhaps you can ask the guide," I suggest.

"He said, 'Open it and it will come to me,' but I still don't get it."

I offered up another suggestion, "Open it to reveal a past lifetime that has a bearing on this lifetime."

"Now I see pictures of an ascending staircase with white, marble, majestic stairs. The stairs are coming out of the book. They are attached at the base but coming out of the book. It could be a castle. I don't know how I fit in here yet. Actually, I'm walking up the stairs. Oh, I see," she said. "You don't read the records; you experience them!"

"I need to live them," she continued, "kind of like a fairy tale. I'm a person. I am wearing a long white dress, and my hair is long and pretty. I have a beautiful golden tiara and a burgundy-colored robe. I am a princess. I can see my face. I'm in my teens. It's 1896 in Bavaria?" She looked quizzical for a moment and then continued. "I'm very regal. I feel safe. I feel like everything is great. It's very light inside, and I have no worries. I'm walking up the stairs. I feel like Rapunzel. Beyond the stairwell, I can see outside, and the landscape is beautiful and very green like Ireland. The doors at the top of the steps are opened for me. Princess Madame. Wow, I'm really pretty! People like me! I don't want to call them servants — they know that I treat them beautifully." Laurie continued to be amazed at how good it felt to be pretty, loved and accepted; something she hadn't experienced in her present lifetime. "They do their job willingly," she continued. "They like me. I'm very kind and gentle and soft spoken. It's so peaceful inside the castle. I'm the light in the castle. The colors are deeper than what my heart feels comfortable with. I'm getting tired and going up the stairs to my boudoir. There are two ladies-in-waiting. Wow, a huge four-poster bed! Most of the bed is white, and it looks so plush and welcoming. I walk into the room, and she removes my royal cloak."

Then Laurie stopped and gasped, "I just heard someone is going to murder me!"

There was a pause, and I waited for Laurie to continue.

"I see my vanity and my dressing table. The servants are just waiting for me to tell them what to do. I'm starting to feel fear and my chambermaid asks if I want tea. I definitely feel fear now. I don't know it in that moment. I really just want to get into bed. My clothes feel pretty, and they don't weigh anything. I don't want to take them off. I just want her to leave. The other lady-in-waiting goes out the door, but she wasn't supposed to use that door. Only I'm allowed to I use that door. She is supposed to use the other door. I can see that she is consorting with the guard. I'm in bed and this lady, my main chambermaid, now looks evil to me. Her eyes are fiery. She's scary now. Why is she looking at me that way? She's wicked and a phony. She was always so nice to me but actually she wanted to poison me with the tea. She doesn't like that the other servants love me because I'm young, beautiful and smart. She hates me! She has children, a daughter she thinks should be in my position. I look at her now, and I know I'm afraid. I'm not moving. I ask her why she's angry. She says I don't deserve to be a princess. But I still don't understand why."

I encouraged Laurie to try to find out why and suddenly she had an "Aha!" moment.

"She says she had an affair with my father, the King, and she feels that he used her. She had an illegitimate child with him, and she feels that her daughter should be the Princess, not me. I try to tell her that my father adores me, but she's raging! I feel her energy. Pure rage! Her eyes are evil! She wants to choke me. It's weird. I'm reading her mind, and I just think my father wouldn't let this happen to me. She had the other lady-in-waiting guard the door. This lady is going to kill me. She wants to kill me too. I can't move . . . or at least, I'm not moving. They both want to kill me. She has nothing, and her daughter has nothing. I ask her how it will benefit her daughter if she kills me. She said the King will let her daughter be a Princess if I'm dead. I say do you really think he is going to love you or your daughter if you kill me? She doesn't care about that. She doesn't believe that anyone will miss me. She chokes me, strangles me! She has a grin on her face and oh my God, she is my mother! I'm dead. She killed me! My mother killed me! I still look pretty even though there are red marks on my neck. She is puffed up like a blowfish and she's happy."

I watched Laurie's face as she relived all of this. It was a lot to experience, and I felt she needed some time to catch her breath.

"I think she realizes it's for naught," Laurie continued after some time had passed. "He's never going to look at her in a positive way. He hates her. He's going to have her killed. She's screaming, 'But I love you!' and then, her head is cut off. Her daughter is there and sees this and feels nothing. She's empty. My dad is so sad. He locks himself away. He knows if he had not been with this woman, I would still be alive. He stays in the tower alone and very sad. He grows a long beard, and he dies. She was jealous of me and couldn't accept my kindness or her position or place in my life. The same is true in this life. She was jealous of me, and she couldn't accept my kindness. She wants me to be her mother next time. She was a chambermaid then, but my mother in this lifetime. She is missing the ability to be kind and gentle and human. I will teach it to her in our next life."

Laurie fully understood her relationship with her mother now. When she opened her eyes, she looked squarely at me and said, "Can you believe that bitch?" Then a second thought came to her, and she added, "And she wants me to be HER mother next time? Ugh." We both laughed. Laurie remained quiet for several seconds while she contemplated what she just experienced. As she departed, a peaceful look came over her face, and I felt her new-found understanding would enable her to begin to forgive her mother after all of these years.

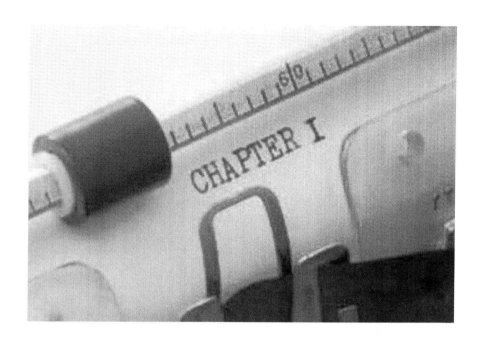

I'm a Novel!

"To literary critics a book is assumed to be guilty until it proves itself innocent."

~ Nelson Algren

Marcus, a British author of two popular novels, came to see me one day. He wanted to write a play this time, but he needed motivation.

He began, "When I wrote my novels in Europe, I saw a hypnotherapist to keep me motivated. But, he's gone now, and I'm looking for someone to help me."

On further exploration, Marcus needed some motivation to achieve his goal of writing the play that was in his mind. His idea centered around an aging gay couple who had lived through years of criticism, hypocrisy and condemnation. According to Marcus, this story needed to be told so people would question outdated attitudes and have a greater understanding of committed relationships of different types.

Marcus had started writing his play but found it to be mostly "rubbish."

"It's not good at all," he lamented, "and I am finding every excuse not to write. Then I find myself in anguish because I didn't write anything all day."

Marcus boasted how he was already accomplished and had proven himself a success to all the people he needed to prove something to his boss, his longtime school buddy, and to himself. There was no financial need to write the play, and since he had already proven his literary skills, there was no reason to write the play at all. Yet here he was looking for motivation to write again.

I saw Marcus several times and noted that at the start of each session, he repeated the same mantra regarding his accomplishments for the first twenty minutes. It became evident that Marcus may have been suffering from a lack of confidence in his abilities.

During our first hypnosis session, Marcus regressed back to writing his university dissertation. It was a very traumatic experience for him as he recalled day-by-day procrastination in writing his paper. Finally on the very last day before the deadline, he forced himself in front of his keyboard and wrote his dissertation to the point of exhaustion. In his words, it was "utter, agonizing pain."

Marcus admitted that his dissertation wasn't very good, but it was good enough to get his degree. The memory of this experience alone was exhausting to Marcus. We moved on to an earlier time in his life where he was able to recall some very positive experiences with his language teacher.

This woman loved Marcus's writing and often had him read his stories to the class. He enjoyed her very much, especially her praise. As he articulated this memory, I carefully anchored this feeling. The feeling of being praised was important, as it would help Marcus to change his state of mind while writing.

Anchors are created when a resourceful state is experienced and is paired with a stimulus. In Marcus's case, writing would become the stimulus. Some anchors happen involuntarily. An example of this would be an old familiar song playing on the radio, or the smell of bread baking in the oven, both of which take you back to a special memory or feeling. Sometimes, anchors work automatically, and you never know what triggered the pairing of the anchor and the stimulus.

Marcus's second session revealed that he now felt better about writing the play, but there was still some resistance. A little voice inside his head kept telling him, "It's no good. People don't talk that way. What I'm writing is rubbish."

Following Marcus's twenty-minute monologue of his accomplishments, I guided him into a trance state. Then, I asked him to explore the initial significant event when he felt a fear of failure.

"I'm six months old," he started, "and I'm being ignored. My brothers are playing. I'm wearing a diaper. I'm in my bedroom on my cot under the porthole. I'm scared of my brothers making fun of me. They were always making fun of me. It's the worst part of being little. I want to merge into the wall so I can't be seen."

Marcus could feel the sense of failure to be significant in his brothers' abusive behavior. Knowing what he knows now, he gently spoke to his little self to heal his inner child.

Next, using an NLP (Neuro-Linguistic Program) technique, I asked Marcus to describe how he pictured his book.

"I see it behind the wall."

Walls are always interesting to me because they often function as large protective shields.

"How big is the wall?" I questioned.

"It is as wide as infinity and just as high," he described.

"And what is it made of?" I questioned.

"It's made of bubbles. It is very pliable. If I push on it, it gives."

I asked him to continue to describe the wall and then I asked if he'd like to remove it.

"No!" He exclaimed: "It protects me from failing. My whole life is a fear of failure. I'd much rather not try something, then to try it and fail. I'm too lazy to slug it out. My whole life I've had a fear of conflict and this wall protects me. It says I'm being pretentious. My writing is rubbish."

"How are you going to reach the book if there is a wall between you and it?" I questioned.

"Well, I would like to cut a hole in the wall, just large enough to reach into it with my arms and write the book like that," Marcus described as his hand came up and he created a large circle in the air.

Suddenly, as Marcus made this gesture, the wall transformed. It was no longer a wall. It became dome-shaped, and it covered the book, much like a glass cake plate cover. Then, it transformed again into an ordinary book with a paper cover.

"It's like the kind of book covers that we used in school to cover a book," Marcus explained.

Then suddenly, the book and the cover were completely gone.

I guided him through his trance state and asked him to see his book.

"It's a small, regular size book. It's red and the cover reads, A Play by Marcus."

I was glad he found the book as it may offer the answers to his fears. I wondered what the book needed from him. In order for Marcus to move forward, it was important to discover what the book needed or wanted.

"Oh, God! I can't believe it," he continued, "it wants to be a novel – not a play! It says it wants to be a novel for its first incarnation. It can have an easy birth that way. It wishes to be a novel. Much less daunting and it wants to not be taken too seriously – more lighthearted – easy birth – it won't feel pretentious that way. It wants to be a comedy because a comedy is not pretentious. Drama is pretentious. It rings true that I'm trying to be something that's not me. I tell it to go away, but part of it wants to badger me, nagging me to be written. It is willing to be more flexible and change. It's accommodating. It needs a commitment. It needs consistency. It needs to be written."

"What does it believe?" I asked.

"It's good. It believes it's very, very good."

A few months had passed before Marcus came back to see me. He was a snowbird who traveled between London to Florida. He had completely stopped writing. After seeing a play in London which had a similar theme to the book he had planned to write, he decided to abandon the idea of writing anything altogether. Now, six months later, he sat in front of me feeling a bit depressed from lack of purpose. "I have everything I have always wanted," he began. "I have had success with my other books. I have always wanted to retire from working and I did. I have a partner with whom I pleased. I am financially secure. But I feel like I'm missing something."

It really wasn't hard to figure out. Not fulfilling your purpose in life is like having ice cream with no spoon to enjoy it. As I looked down at my notes, I realized that he may need to see his book of life in the Akashic Records in order to find the motivation to get back to writing.

He went into a trance easily.

"I'm in the Hall of Records. It's a huge room filled with rows and rows of books that go to a ceiling that goes really high up. Really high. It feels like I'm in a Harry Potter movie." I've heard many accounts by my clients of a dark wooded, great hall, all having a similar appeal, as they describe the Akashic Hall of Records.

I suggested someone would come to guide him to his records, and sure enough he saw a man walking up to him. It was a man in a black suit.

"It looks like my father," he said. "Wait... It is my father."

Family members are often present when my clients visit the Hall of Records. We worked with what Marcus was experiencing. There were no messages from his father, and his father was not his guide. His mother came into the room as well, but no guide appeared. Marcus located his records by himself.

"It's high up. I see it, but I'm not able to reach it," he began.

"Ask for help," I offered and suddenly he floated up until he was able to reach his book of life.

"It's quite beautiful. Gold bound," Marcus said. It had no name on it, but he knew it was his.

"What would you like to ask it? Your book has the answers to all of life's questions."

"I'd like to ask it how long I will live." The answer seemed to satisfy him: 81 years.

"Is there any meaning or purpose for my life?" The answer came immediately as well as a smile on his face. "It says my purpose is to write."

He continued aloud, "Am I going to write again and will my work be published?"

I waited to hear the answer.

"Yes. It said yes." Marcus told me. "A novel - then a play." He continued with more questions, "Will I remain financially independent?" and suddenly he was walking into a theatre with many people waving to him.

The Akashic records can answer in many different ways. In this instance, Marcus experienced the answers as he suddenly found himself experiencing his future in this lifetime. "I am at a performance. I'm at my play. I'm in London at the theatre. Lots of people I know are here. There are parties afterwards and I'm at a party for the cast and producers. It's a bit stressful. Good stress though. I'm happy. I'm enjoying this. The reviews come out late at night – early morning. They are mixed. But it's good overall."

As we ended the session, Marcus was well pleased with his experience having gone into the Akashic records. "This is one for the memory books!" He said. He was genuinely excited to begin working on his play again. His plan was to start on it the very next morning. I look forward to reading his play.

The Healer

*The state of ill health is a moment to moment
happening. Healing is moment to moment balance,
bringing awareness to our thoughts, feelings and
emotions and how we respond.*

~ Vasant Lad, Ayurvedic Healing

A beautiful young woman with long dark hair visited my office one day. She found my website while performing an Internet search for information about Dr. Brian Weiss. My website contains specific information regarding my teacher, Dr. Weiss.

"I feel a connection with you, and I know that I have some unresolved issues that may have come from a past life." Vallory was attending college to become a nurse, and whenever she took a test, she was riddled with anxiety. "I can't understand it," she said. "I study really hard, and I know the material, but I just feel like I might not get the answers right. I might do it wrong." Her brows furrowed as her beautiful face filled with anguish. "I also find myself waking up at night filled with anxiety. I get up out of bed and do some work, but it doesn't seem to help. I feel like I'm worried, but I don't specifically know what I'm worried about."

I performed a hypnotic induction, and within moments, Vallory had gone into a deep trance. Her eyelids fluttered, and her legs twitched. Her first memory from childhood emerged.

"I am playing with my sister. We are in the backyard, and we're trying to catch the pretty butterflies." She began describing the scene. "It's odd, I can see her and me playing, and I remember this happening, but my sister passed away shortly after she was born. But yet it is so clear, here and now, as I'm experiencing this. My mother is looking at me through the window. She worries about me constantly."

Vallory's connection to her deceased sister wasn't unusual to me. When children enter this physical world and spiritually detach from the other side, they are still very much connected to spiritual energy, as the detachment is more gradual than fully understood. Seeing or speaking to someone on the other side is sometimes easy for young children as they have no preconceived notions about someone who has died.

Moving her along, I suggested that we continue with our mind journey and go back to the time while in her mother's womb. This period was very pleasant for Vallory because she had very loving parents. Then we continued onward into the past to possibly learn about lifetimes that may have had a bearing on her current one.

"I'm wearing sandals," Vallory began. She was a young Native American girl riding a beautiful horse in this past life. Her sister was behind her, and they were laughing together. This was the same sister, who had died shortly after birth in her present lifetime, that she saw herself playing with as a child. Suddenly the horse bucked, and her little sister was thrown off. Vallory, upset by this, started crying. Her sister passed very early in that lifetime as well. I wanted to know if this was the cause of Vallory's anxiety.

We continued with the regression.

"I have a needle in my hand," Vallory told me. "I'm male, and I'm wearing scrubs, but not the same scrubs as the nurses. I'm a doctor. There's a bright light. I'm operating on someone's stomach, and I'm worried. It's over, and I am pacing the halls. I am waiting for the results because they matter very much to me. I know my patient. He's my father. I operated on my father. I'm worried because I just feel like I might not have gotten it right. I might have done it wrong."

I'd heard these words before. It was the same words Vallory used to describe how she felt when she was taking an exam. Here in a different lifetime, Vallory was a male surgeon who was ordinarily very confident. However, while operating on his father, he became anxious and worried that he might have done something wrong and possibly jeopardized his father's life. But, as it turned out, he had done it right. Vallory now saw why she had so much anxiety about doing things 'right.' The relief showed on her face as she took a deep breath and awakened. "I feel so much lighter," she said as she sat up to talk about the regression.

In the post discussion, Vallory was amazed at the memory of herself and her little sister catching butterflies. "My mom was surprised when she learned she was pregnant with me," she volunteered. "She had previously lost her little girl. Her name was Amber. That's really weird. She lost her when she was two months old. My sister had a bowel disorder. Her small intestine was wrapped around her large intestine. She died in my mother's arms at the hospital." Vallory looked down into her emotions.

She continued, "One month later, my mother was pregnant with me. The odd thing was, she and my dad were too upset to have sex, so they don't know how I was conceived. But, yet, here I am!"

I believed strongly in the Akashic records, and I knew she could find the answers there. Vallory made another appointment, and we hugged goodbye.

Upon her return, Vallory explained that her anxiety had lessened, but her intuition became almost acute. "I not only seem to know things, but I see them before they happen. I saw my fiancé getting ready for work, but he was still right next to me. I can't really explain it. Oh, and also, one night when I was sleeping, my body was still, but somehow I rose above it. I felt like I was floating and looking down at my body and my fiancé. It was so strange."

This happens sometimes when one starts to open up to the spiritual world. Their senses heighten, and they become more attuned to the energy around them. As for rising above her body, this is known as astral projection. One can literally separate their astral body from their physical body and have an out-of-body experience.

Vallory continued talking excitedly. "Oh, and I went to visit my mom. I told her all about my experience with you. She said I always loved horses. In fact, when I was a little girl I always drew pictures of a girl with long dark braids wearing a Native

American outfit, and with a white and black horse. It was always the same horse, hair, and outfit. I would even draw pictures for my teachers and girlfriends." I noted this information and asked if there was something in particular she would like to focus on. Vallory was still stressed out about nursing school. She was unsure if she wanted to continue with this school, or whether she should go for her RN or PA. If she did follow the path of an RN, what nursing discipline should she pursue: ER nurse, child pediatric nurse, anesthesiology, or a nurse who works with cancer patients? She also mentioned that she would like to open her own small business. She was interested in doing something related to healing.

We talked a bit more about Vallory's feelings and aspirations, and then I decided to perform a guided meditation with her. I wanted to take Vallory to a beautiful garden containing colorful flowers and plants, with fluttering butterflies to allow her superconscious mind to engage future events. And perhaps during this guided trance to the garden, loved ones would come visit and offer her some answers. Vallory entered a deep trance very quickly. When no others entered the garden, I guided her to the Akashic records.

"I am holding a big brown book," she told me. "The edges are gold, and inside it, there are many pictures of me. They're moving pictures. I see short little clips of me doing things in nature, such as hiking, or backpacking. It is so strange because the pictures are like mini videos that last about 30 seconds or so, and then they stop and repeat.

In the next scene, I am in a white coat, a nurse lab coat at a hospital. I look really tired. I'm sitting down to take a break. I look exhausted. It is the emergency room, and I just got done with surgery. I sit down and put my face in my hands. The scene ends. In the next picture, I am talking with my fiancé. I am saying I don't connect with my patients. They come and go so quickly. I don't get to see them again. Everything is so fast." Vallory's face became sullen, so I moved her along by asking her if there was another way to heal others.

"I see another scene. In this one, I'm happy. I'm holding hands with many of my patients. They love me. They ask for me. I'm holding hands with different people. I am in a different kind of hospital setting." Wanting to know more and get a clearer picture of her life, I asked her to go to her graduation day. "I'm there. I'm in a cap and gown."

"Take a look at your Diploma. What school is it from?" I knew Vallory was enrolled at Broward Nursing College, but very unhappy with the school and feeling anxiety about it, so I thought it might be interesting to know if there was a college better suited for her.

"It says, 'Miami-Dade School of Nursing.' It's an RN degree. September 2015."

What was interesting about this is that I asked her to go into the records and find the best school for her, so I wasn't surprised that the records showed a different nursing college. Vallory had expressed interest in knowing if she was going to open a small healing practice, so I decided to push forward to see if she owned such a business. Perhaps she had a business card with her.

"It's in the pocket of my lab coat," she said. "It has my name on it with RN and a symbol made up of a circle, a flower and three leaves inside it. I can see my name along with some letters I don't recognize underneath it."

I asked her to speak the letters and any markings that she recognized.

"A-Y-R-U-D-E-I-C Medicine," she spoke. Then she read some more, "September 2015. And I see my ID card from Miami-Dade Hospital Trauma Center. There is another card here too, a smaller one. It is also an ID Badge. It says Holy Cross. I work at a part of the hospital I don't recognize. My ID badge says Alternative Healer. And under that, I see the same letters only this time they are much clearer. A-Y-U-R-V-E-D-I-C. 2017."

I had not heard of this particular type of healing before, so I made a note to look this up after the session.

Vallory suddenly found herself in a past life. This sometimes happens when important information is needed to explain answers to life's questions. "I see Ryan. He is my ex-lover. We are in a different lifetime together, and we are married. It's a healthy relationship, but now I see that I spent my whole life taking care of him. He needed help, and I was the only one who understood him. We had two children. I chase them out of the room. I don't want them to see how sick he is."

Her next scene took her into the future. Brian (her fiancé) was waiting for her. "It's five years from now. I see a green house with a porch. It's further out in a wooded area. It might be Florida. There are tons of flowers everywhere and land, and there's a black and white horse. The backyard is unbelievable. It's filled with plants and wildlife. There are people sitting in a circle, and someone is leading them in mediation. I am inside the house in the kitchen looking out the window and journaling. The date on my journal is 2-27-2019. I am still a nurse; I see my nursing stuff on the counter ready to go. I'm on call, but I'm not tired. I'm relaxed and not at all stressed about my job."

I asked about her family.

"A little girl just ran into the house and gave me a big hug. I'm doing alternative healing. My house is filled with plants, flowers, and candles. Brian works in radiation therapy for an oncologist. He is asking if I would be able to help the little girl with her medical condition and could I schedule an appointment."

I decided that this would be a good time for Vallory to see exactly how she facilitates healing. I asked her to go to the time of that appointment with the little girl.

"I am holding the little girl's hands. I put her feet in water and wash them. There is a table. I'm preparing her to get up on the table. She is wearing a white robe. I put my hands above her eyes, and I move them around over her entire body. She is glowing. She looks calmer. She came from Baltimore, and her family is with her. They are thanking me."

I asked her what the little girl's illness was.

"She had cancer. But now she doesn't. She is glowing."

Since she was going to facilitate healings, then perhaps she had "earned" the capacity to heal during a past lifetime. Karma is the balancing of energy. A full accounting of every action and reaction is recorded in the Akashic Records. It's the universe's perfect accounting system, and the universe has its own timing for all energetic actions. From our conversation before the hypnosis session, I wanted Vallory to see a past lifetime that may have had a significant impact on her current lifetime.

"I'm on a creek playing with a bunch of young boys." Vallory was being shown a past life. "I'm swinging on a rope. I let go and splash in the water. My mom is calling me. My sandals are on the shore. They're soaking wet, and I know my mom is going to be angry. I have a black and white horse, and I'm scurrying around to get home quickly."

I ask her for her name, and she indignantly answers as if I should already know it.

"Everyone knows I'm Pocahontas!"

Not knowing much about the history of Pocahontas, except what I remember of the Disney films, I asked her to go to a significant event. This was a unique occurrence for me that someone was experiencing a past life as relevant as Vallory was now experiencing. Until now, past life regressions had not been with famous or even infamous people.

"I am on a mountain. Two sides are against each other. They all have weapons - on one side are the people from an Indian tribe and the other more modernized. I am in the middle. I am talking, offering peaceful advice. They are listening. They are stopping, and there's an exchange of two men, a small bag of coins, and a headpiece with feathers and beads. There are modernized people living close to our land. The children play together (smiling now) I see the Indian children and the modern children running around."

I advised her to go to the end of that lifetime to find out more about the lessons she'd learned.

"I was the peacemaker. I am in a box surrounded by flowers." Floating above her deceased body, she continued, "I am surrounded by animals. Everyone is speaking the same language. There are deer here and birds. It's a magical scene. I've never seen anything like this before. It's the prettiest place." I let her continue to enjoy the experience briefly as I could see her face glowing, and I knew she was communicating with the animals. It is always crucial with this kind of work to allow the client time to learn a lesson from a past life. "My lesson is to let go of trying to control. Let go of money and other people's perception of what to do."

While she remained in her trance state, I asked if she had something more that she needed to share. With that, she asked for a paper and pen, and she sat quietly writing fervently. Here is what she wrote:

Everyone has a spirit guide. My guide is Mother Mary. She is a guide for all women, actually. She has insight that men who are Masters do not have, and she can intervene whenever she pleases to change the course of events. She has complete control over our Akashic Records. The animals and nature are in perfect balance. They never give too much or take too much; they know what we must learn as humans. They are the happiest living things on this earth, and since we cannot communicate with them directly through language, we must work to understand their pure energy in order to receive knowledge from them. Their energy is completely balanced. Mother Mary and God and the Masters are all connected. The Masters are God & Mother Mary's helpers. That's why the Akashic Record Room has an open ceiling. They watch over the Masters, and they guide them.

When Vallory returned to full waking state, she peered through her wide-open brown eyes. She was amazed! She was in awe! Neither one of us had ever heard of the Ayurvedic healing, so I turned to my computer. An Internet search revealed that in-fact there was such a healing process. On the Ayurvedic Institute it states:

Ayurveda, the science of life, is an ancient art of healing that has been practiced continuously throughout India for over 5,000 years. Ayurvedic healing includes herbs, nutrition, panchakarma cleansing, acupressure massage, Yoga, Sanskrit, and Jyotish (Vedic astrology). Certification is offered to become an Ayurvedic Practitioner.

Vallory looked at my computer screen and gasped. Right in front of her was the exact same logo she saw on her card. It was the three-leaf symbol used for Ayurvedic Institute. We were both shocked.

When Vallory began her next session with me, I immediately guided her to the Akashic Records Room. "A man with a white beard and a walking stick is handing me my book. He wants me to sit. It is the same place I've been before. He wants me to sit down. It's okay for me to open my book now. I open the book. It is taking me to the very first pages of the book. I see the picture of an eye."

I waited to find out what the eye in the book meant to Vallory.

"It looks like my eye. It is just the picture of one eye and it's damaged. The man with the white beard is sitting on the edge of the bench now and is showing me how the eye healed, and he's pointing to the sky. There is no ceiling in the room. It's open just like last time when the stars were showing. He is pointing to me now, and I'm flipping through the pages. This section of the book has pictures of parts of my body that were damaged. He wants me to flip through these photographs. I think I understand. I think they have healed these things for me. They healed all these things that were wrong with me at some point and quickly, too. I want to say thank you, but he keeps shaking his head, 'no.' It's not him. He's pointing at me. We are just sitting there, but he seems aggravated that I haven't been writing things down. I can move on now, and I am glad because some pictures are kind of gruesome. There are many pictures of my stomach. There's blackness around my intestines."

This made perfect sense to me because Vallory had told me during my initial assessment of her that she suffered from

Irritable Bowel Syndrome (IBS) which is a gastrointestinal (GI) disorder.

"The pictures take me through the healing process," she continued. "The sick area is black, and the light comes and takes the darkness away. Now the man is getting up. His hand is on my shoulder, and he asks me if I understand. I tell him I'm pretty sure that I do. He doesn't speak, but I know what he is asking me. There's a pink rose that just appeared on the table. I asked about the healing, and it seems I am healed directly through them, especially Mother Mary. Other people can't get to them like I can. They tell me I'm going to use herbs and a new energy healing for patients to get into contact with their healing guides. He is saying that people have too many blocks, and it is better to heal outside of the hospital. There are too many blocks inside the hospital. My sensitivity is what makes me understand this. They said I'm going to work with really sick people. Some will stay. Some will go. If they go, I will heal them in a way which will let them be okay with the process. I am going to need to protect myself. One way to heal is through my thoughts. When my dog Bella puts her head near my heart, she is doing it for a reason. Only animals can do this. That's Bella's way. It is for both of us. Praying is supposed to help me with healing but in a different way. In the book, I see myself in a few pictures traveling to distant places and gathering plants. I'm speaking to someone in a tribe about the plants. I am with my fiancé, Brian. We are backpacking."

I asked her to ask about the healing, and she responded with, "It seems the first time I meet a client I will be counseling them on nutrition and exercise. I don't heal the way I want to until I get through a few sessions. I learn Reiki. I feel through nature, the beach, water, and I'm trying to ask what healing it is. There is no name. He is showing me now that I'm putting my hands over them, and I am using water as well. My hands are slightly above or on the skin. I wash my hands in a bowl near me, and the water is blessed. I put my hands over the water and just say a prayer to bless the water. There is one person who has a medical wraparound. The wrap was in the water and I take the wrap out and place it around where the person needs it. I wash their feet with the water. It draws out all the impurities. I awaken them. Before I do the energy healing, I put them through a light hypnosis. The Masters told me I do that, so the person totally relaxes. Then I can see their energy. I use oil on their temples, hands, feet and other areas. I can teach some things, but I can't teach direct healing."

"Do you know why you received the gift of healing?" I asked her.

"It's what Mother Mary wants," she told me. "Mother Mary is the pink rose on the table."

"Can the Masters tell us more about cancer?" I asked Vallory.

"They're telling me that cancer is a result of the body's continued and prolonged exposure to stressful conditions. We all have cancer cells in our bodies for proper balance of normal healthy cells, but they are exceedingly sensitive. They are beneficial to our bodies but are easily disrupted. Once disrupted, they multiply beyond their normal rate and find a way to survive by killing other healthy cells. Our understanding is limited from a medical standpoint, and our technology merely permits us to determine when cancer cells develop, and how far they have spread. Western practitioners don't fully understand the full cause and effect of cancer. They don't understand how to help a person de-stress before cancer begins."

Two years later, Vallory graduated from Miami-Dade Nursing School with a Registered Nursing Degree. Since counseling

Vallory through hypnosis, past life regression and the Akashic records, it has been my sincere wish that one day I will come in contact with her again to learn where her path may have led her in the aftermath of her extraordinary sessions.

I Can't Pick Up A Pen!

"Have you ever met someone for the first time, but in your heart you feel as if you've met them before?"

~ JoAnne Kenrick, When A Mullo Loves A Woman

The wife of a famous author found my website on the Internet one day and called me. "I'm blocked, and I need some help." Celeste came to my office the following week. Clients often call me when they feel like their lives are not moving forward. Sometimes they need to move on from a negative relationship, change careers, or just find out what their life's purpose is. Celeste explained that she had authored books with her husband and had written many forewords for other authors.

"I know there is a book in me. It is waiting to be written, and I want to write it, but I can't even pick up a pen. I'm stuck!"

Before I begin the hypnotic part of a session, I always ask my clients to state an intention for the session. Celeste had three. The first was to understand her connection to her husband better. "When we first met, he was visiting at the building where I worked. I didn't know who he was. I walked past him as he was standing in a throng of people, and I scurried into my office. I was startled when he appeared right behind me. 'Do you know what day it is today?' he asked. 'It's Valentine's Day, and I have a heart on for you!' Then he pointed to a cute little red heart pinned to his lapel. I looked in his eyes and immediately I knew our destiny. I turned bright red and spun around quickly so he wouldn't see. We dated and were married shortly after that."

Celeste's second goal was to better understand her 'gift of writing.' She could write for others and with others, but she struggled to write her own material.

Her third goal was to understand why her current lifetime seemed to embody so many rewards. "I have everything I've ever wanted including a large family." Celeste had many children, and she was proud to be a hands-on mom to all of them.

Celeste's trance state came quickly to her. "I see a huge stone building, tall doors, a dirt floor, and dirt roads. It's daytime, and I am walking. I have no shoes on. It's a hospital, and I hear sounds of agony. It's during a war. There are people who have been injured in a battle, but not just soldiers. Gershwin Hospital. I work there. I'm a nun. I hold patients' hands." Celeste suddenly saw her husband. "There he is! He's a patient. He's in a hospital bed with a sheet covering him. Nothing can be done to save his life. He's calm, and I'm holding his hand while saying a prayer. He does not want to die, but I'm comforting him and telling him to let go. His breathing changes. His breaths become shallower now, and I know he doesn't have much time left. He wants to believe in God, but he doesn't. He needs proof. He reminds me of war. I remind him of the good things in life, like the trees and the sky. He's sobbing now, and he's exasperated with me. I have a cross made out of wood, and I give it to him."

"'There's no power in that,' he says as he holds it. 'War is from God. I've seen too much.' But I tell him, 'No. War is from man. Until we love and accept each other, it will be this way.' He has no family. His parents were killed. He is a young man, perhaps only 17 or 18 years old and he dies."

Celeste's next significant event occurred in a jail cell.

"It is very light in here. There are bars on the windows. I am still a nun, and I am holding children on my lap. I need to protect them. I'm overwhelmed. I see my hands. I have no thumbs. I wrote about love and acceptance, and the powers that be cut off my thumbs. They didn't like what I was writing. Suddenly there is a bright light, like an explosion. Everything disappears, and we all die."

I encouraged her to follow her soul to the afterlife. "I see my grandmother. She is here. My life's purpose was to promote peace and love. Everyone can have it."

Now I understood why Celeste couldn't pick up a pen. I offered the suggestion that her writing was a problem for the establishment in a past lifetime. In this lifetime, it is safe to promote peace, love, and acceptance.

Offering her a posthypnotic suggestion, I said, "In this life, you have thumbs, and your thumbs allow you to hold a pen to write the story that is within you. When you begin to write your story, you will be amazed at how effortlessly the words will flow onto the paper, in an almost divine nature."

At Celeste's next appointment, she said she felt strongly that what she'd experienced under trance was real. "The images and the experience I had while in hypnosis at first seemed like just my imagination, but it's still there. It's a concrete image, and I don't think that I could have conjured it up in my mind. If it had only been a figment of my imagination, I don't believe that I would feel such a profound sense that this surely happened."

Clients who experience a past life during their session often feel the desire to go deeper into the spiritual realm. It's an entirely different dimension that unlocks their understanding that there is more here than we are aware of. In her past life, she was a nun. Her life was spent praying and consoling young soldiers who were about to cross over. Her belief in God was resolute, and her life's purpose was to promote peace and love, to show everyone that they can experience it. However, during that period of time with significant political and social unrest, her message was denounced, and her thumbs cut off. That left me curious to find out what we would learn together during our next session.

Before we began, I asked her to set a goal for the session. Celeste's intentions were to find the purpose of her current life and to know her future.

Just as she'd experienced in her previous session, Celeste entered a deep trance almost immediately. As I described the pathway for her to follow, her countenance lightened, and the twitching of her eyelids signaled that she was ready to enter the Akashic Records. I never know who will join my client once they're inside the Hall of Records, although family members often make a showing. Usually, it is the librarian or guide, an old man with a long white beard and wrinkled hands holding an elaborately carved staff and dressed in a white robe. Sometimes it is someone they know, someone who has passed, or a spiritual guide. In Celeste's experience, it was a man in biblical clothing, a man wearing a red velvet jacket, and an ornate crown, with tights, and large wings on his back. I wasn't sure where she was as I had never heard that description before, but I quickly learned that she was in the Library of Records as she described her surroundings. "There are high shelves everywhere I look, and the books are on shelves that are very tall. There are stone tablets that are gorgeous; pink, beige and white marble tablets."

I asked her to follow her guide to her book of life. It took a while, but she followed him, and he handed her a large book with a green cover and gold lettering inscribed, 'The Mother.' This couldn't be mine," she insisted and then smiled. He said, 'Yes, it's yours.'"

Without prompting, she continued. "I am being told to bring the purpose of children back to purity. I should allow God to work from within. I will write about it to awaken mothers' consciousness about why they are bringing forth a child into this world. There are so many children being born to people without consciousness. I want to teach a different way."

"My mother and my grandmother are here. There are many people from my past. My father is here as well. This is weird because he is still alive and has Alzheimer's. My mother is saying she always saw the Divine in me." Celeste smiled. "My guide is the Archangel Michael. He is telling me I will be given the information for my book in time. He is showing me my life with my husband. It's a beautiful life. My husband stands behind me when I'm speaking and sharing my insights with an audience."

I find it so intriguing when we are given answers to questions that have not even been asked yet. I watched as Celeste's expression changed. She was obviously listening intently to what was being said. I questioned her about what she was experiencing.

"He's telling me not to be stressed. He knows I've been stressed about the plane that's gone missing." Eleven days prior to our session, on March 8th, 2014, the Malaysian Airlines Flight 370 had suddenly disappeared. A worldwide search to locate this plane began, but as of March 19th, the day of our session, investigators were still empty-handed. They didn't know when the aircraft's transponder and ACARS systems were turned off, and they were forced to speculate where the plane could be.

"The plane is in water," Celeste apprised me. "It's in the water, and the plane is intact. It's in the Indian Ocean. I can see it. It's on the floor of the ocean intact. There was an electrical failure. The electrical system completely shut down. The pilot was able to guide the plane onto the top of the water. We won't find it for a while. He is saying something with the pilot. Something with the pilot, but I don't know."

I wasn't sure about Celeste, but I was completely blown away. We had not discussed this topic before, and she had not identified this as a goal when we began our session. I didn't know why we were receiving this information.

Celeste was quiet for a few moments and then suddenly added, "I'm told it is the way it is and to have peace about it."

"It's for you," she continued. "The information is for your book. It's for you."

I thanked Archangel Michael for this information and said a silent prayer for the loved ones and for those who died.

A few weeks later I heard from Celeste. She told me that she was now writing daily and had already completed 25 pages of her book.

It is worth mentioning as a side note, at the time of this writing, it had been reported that airline debris was found on a beach in Saint-André, on Reunion, an island in the western Indian Ocean. It was believed to be a portion of a right wing from a Boeing 777 and to have been Malaysian Airlines Flight 370.

According to the International Business Times:

Zaaim Redha Abdul Rahma, who took part in the initial search for the plane, said the state of the debris indicated that the plane likely landed in the ocean and floated for some time before sinking, rather than crashing violently into the water. The flaperon's condition indicated it likely sat for some time at the bottom of the ocean with the plane before detaching and being pulled to shore by currents, he added. Some have speculated that it might indicate the plane is still sitting intact on the Indian Ocean floor.

I'm an Alcoholic!

"Before you can live a part of you has to die. You have to let go of what could have been, how you should have acted and what you wish you would have said differently. You have to accept that you can't change your past experiences, opinions of others at that moment in time, or outcomes from their choices or yours. When you finally recognize that truth, then you will understand the true meaning of forgiveness of yourself and others. From this point, you will finally be free."

~ Shannon L. Alder

"I'm an alcoholic," Bob began. "My father was an alcoholic, my grandfather was an alcoholic, and his father was one, too. It runs in the family."

Addictions have a strong hold on people. Whether it is an addiction to cigarettes, food, or alcohol, clients tend to believe that the tentacles of addiction are too long and too strong to escape from. In this case, Bob believed it was hereditary. Bob wanted to retire from his computer business and continue teaching Tai Chi and meditation. He knew that his addiction was getting in the way, but he wasn't sure how to conquer it.

"I don't drink to the point where I am hung over badly, like an old person. It's just for me, I need freedom from it because I teach mediation and Tai Chi and these types of martial arts require me to have a clear mind to really give the best of myself to my clients; not to mention my family."

"It may be a subconscious fear of success or living the dream that forces me to hold myself back. I don't have a conscious fear of it. I have a beautiful house, family life, two daughters and a successful computer business, but that's not the kind of success I'm looking for. I want that spiritual success where every moment I feel connected to Source. I have had glimpses, but I'd like to be more connected."

Before visiting the Akashic Records, I asked Bob to formulate at least two questions or goals. In this case, Bob wanted to know if his current desire to make Tai Chi teaching his career would enable his soul to reach its fullest potential in this lifetime, and he also wanted to know the source of his issue with alcohol, his dependency, and his tendency to binge.

I performed an induction and Bob gradually relaxed. I guided him to the Akashic Records Library where Bob was in awe of the size and the rows and rows of tall shelves filled with books. He located his guide, a librarian who brought his book to him.

"It's mahogany leather with gold inlaid strips," he described and then elaborated, "and at the bottom is the Roman numeral

IV. I think this is the 4th book in a series, but I don't know what the series is."

A peek into his Book of Life sent him in the direction of his future, and gave him the guidance he was looking for. The records offer the experience of different paths one could take. One, continue drinking or two, make a different decision. It also shows us past lifetimes where similar experiences were endured and the results that occurred as a consequence. This permits us to have free will to make wiser decisions that will enhance the rest of this lifetime.

"I am at a beautiful beach with my wife. We are sitting on the sand, and it's a beautiful sunny day. We are watching Valerie, our daughter, as she is playing in the shallow water with her daughter. The child is our grandchild. She is about two years old." Bob's oldest daughter was presently 12 years old, so I knew he was experiencing a future scene.

"It is truly an idyllic setting," he continued. "We are in Hawaii, and I feel we live here, at least part of the year. We're so happy and at peace. I sense this is where I, where 'we' can be if I pursue Tai Chi, being led by my heart, and having intentions to pursue selfless service to others."

He paused and took a breath. A look of confusion crossed his face.

"Now I'm somewhere else. It seems to be Ireland or Scotland. Near the ocean where there is very gray weather with a lot of drizzly, misty rain. I can see the ocean waves crashing on the rocks, partially covered with grass or moss. There is a tower on a hill on the ocean, kind of like a castle. It's a building made of gray stone. I feel like it is the 1500's or 1600's. I move back a little in time, and I see bars. I'm in prison, and I've been in prison for a long time and will be in prison for a long time to come. I committed some sort of financial fraud type of crime. It was nothing violent, but still it was very wrong. Now I'm a lonely, lonely man."

Without prompting, Bob went to yet another era and another lifetime.

"It seems to be gladiator-like times. I see a wagon. I have many servants, both men and women. I am a very powerful man, and I'm full of anger. I whip my servants. I get pleasure from inflicting pain on others. I'm a rich and powerful man, and everything that I have was gained through the domination of others. I'm always angry. It feels like I'm angry about something that happened when I was a child. I'm not sure what happened, but I'm still angry because of it. I used what happened when I was young to justify my anger and domination and torture of others. I have a very large home or estate, but no wife or children. But there are plenty of women around to give me pleasure. I die a poor homeless man on the streets. As soon as I could no longer dominate others physically, I lost everything that I had. As I never loved anyone or had a wife and family, I died a lonely, lonely man."

I ask what there is to learn from these lifetimes.

"It's all a choice. Everything is a choice. Good, bad, indifferent. It's all a choice."

I suggested that he return to the records. At the door to the Hall of Records, Bob is met by a Master. "He tells me I must be true to what I've been taught. I must always be authentic with my Tai Ji Quan each and every day, each and every moment. I've been blessed with this gift of knowledge. I must be true to myself and the teachings. As long as I am true to myself and follow my heart, all will end well."

Bob then saw himself flying. "I'm zooming up and away, like Superman. I'm flying fast! I want to follow, but my feet are heavy." I had no idea where he was flying to, but our session was almost over, and I wanted to bring him back to a sound state of consciousness. It took a while, and I could see in his glassy eyes that he was still mystified. He made me smile when he turned to me and said, "There's nothing like being in a divine state of mind." We both laughed and since the wording was so succinct, I decided to use it as my book title with my client's permission of course.

In a post-session discussion, Bob came to the realization that the two lifetimes ended as they did because of very poor choices. "They were all my choices and my decisions. Even when I was the powerful, angry man, I made a choice to inflict pain on others. It was my choice to hold onto the anger and pain from a negative childhood experience. I chose to alleviate the pain by inflicting pain on others. Alcohol is like that for me in this lifetime. No matter how long or how hard I search, I will not find one particular event, in this or any other lifetime, that is specifically causing me to drink. It's all a choice. In other lifetimes, I chose other sinful things that slowed or stopped the evolution of my soul. In this lifetime, I'm choosing alcohol."

Bob still had a mystified look in his eyes as he continued sharing his thoughts.

"It was always my choice, and it will always be my choice. As such, I can simply CHOOSE not to let alcohol impede my evolution. I can choose not to let alcohol prevent me from experiencing paradise. It isn't that complicated. It's quite simple, actually. IT IS ALL MY CHOICE. If I continue to choose the alcohol, I will very likely die a lonely, lonely man, even if I'm surrounded by people who love me. When I die, I will be completely alone inside mentally and spiritually. But I can easily choose the right path. If I follow my heart into a Tai Chi career serving others, it is possible for me to experience paradise in this lifetime on this earth. If I choose the path that's been shown to me, the path that would elevate my soul, and that path that I know is right for me, I can experience paradise on this earth in this lifetime. It is all up to me. It's all my choice. I could choose to experience Heaven on Earth."

I could not have said it better. Bob was able to see the truth about his choices through his experience with the Akashic Records. Understanding how his decisions during his past lives affected his overall happiness, Bob was able to decide for himself where his behavior might lead him in this lifetime if he continued to drink. Seeing how it was possible to live in a paradise on earth by making different choices made it clear and presented him with an easy decision to make that lifestyle change.

I met with Bob a year later. He came back to have a deeper connection with Source. Bob was happy to report that after our last session, he was able to come to terms with his drinking and was enjoying moving forward on his spiritual path.

The Tree House

"I want to write, but more than that, I want to bring out all kinds of things that lie buried deep in my heart."

~ Anne Frank, The Diary of a Young Girl

A demure woman walked into my office and flopped into the chair. "I'm exhausted," she said. "I'm 43, and I have a 17-month-old baby girl named Annie." She paused for a moment to think, "Need I say more?" She laughed. She really didn't need to elaborate, and for the moment that was all I needed to hear. Sofia was a gentle soul who looked like life was taxing her. She was an understated beauty with placid blue eyes that revealed an inner pain that could never be assuaged. She had a quiet demeanor, and with a soft voice she explained how her two best friends, sisters no less, both died years ago when they were all in their early teens. "They were everything to me. We had so much fun together. We grew up together, and I loved them dearly. Then during high school one of the sisters, Gretchen, was killed in an automobile accident. One year after that, her sister Sigrid was struck by a car and also died. I was a mess. I couldn't go to school, and I didn't want to leave the house. The pain of losing them was almost unbearable."

I let her continue because I could see her pain and knew she had more to say.

"I'm tired and angry all the time, and I'm filled with anxiety over my daughter. My fears are irrational at times, and I'm afraid that my daughter and I might die even when we're perfectly safe, and I know it. I have no self-worth because I was raised in a very dysfunctional family. Can you help me?" She had tears streaming down her face.

Sofia admitted that she was struggling with depression and anxiety due to thirty years of unresolved grief from the loss of her two dearest friends. I decided to perform a guided meditation and lead her to a beautiful garden to perhaps see if she would meet up her two sister friends again. While in a 'divine state of mind', the superconscious mind opens and allows the energy of the souls who have crossed over to visit with us. Perhaps this was how Sofia had located me. Maybe she was guided.

"I had a dream," she continued before we started. "I was in a field with deer and flowers, and I died. But even after I was dead, nothing had changed. I was still in that field, although it was a peaceful place, and it was even more beautiful after I had died." Sometimes dreams provide answers to our fears. In this instance, she was shown that death is a peaceful change of existence.

We spoke for a while longer and then began the hypnotic session with an induction. She plunged deeply into a trance state. Going deeper and deeper, she began describing the beautiful majestic garden with violet flowers that she saw through her mind's eye. Sofia didn't feel alone in the garden. She sensed someone or something was with her there. Her facial expressions said it all. She was connecting with someone.

After a gentle smile appeared on her face, Sofia became emotional and tears streamed down her face. "They're here! Both of them are here! I can see them! They're so real. Sigrid is older. She was such a sweet person. She says it's time to end the turmoil that I feel. She's telling me, 'See yourself as whole.'" Then Sofia began laughing. "She said I should go and get some Prozac!" Laughing again, "And gain some weight. I'm too skinny. A part of them is in my daughter. Sigrid and Gretchen are the same even though they're sisters. They wanted to be together. So Sigrid followed shortly after Gretchen left. They're together because they're one soul. They brought Richard to me (her current husband) and they're always around. They have bodies and hands; they're whole!"

Sofia explained later that Gretchen had been dismembered in the car accident that took her life. This had always bothered Sofia subconsciously and seeing Gretchen whole again with arms and legs was a big part of the healing process for her.

"Look!" She told me, "They have arms and legs. They're showing me that their bodies are whole again." Sofia wept. "Gretchen's body was destroyed in the accident." Overwrought with emotion now as if 28 years of grief was released in a single moment, Sofia was balling now.

It was life transforming. Sofia had been carrying around this grief for the better part of her adult life. She feared death through dismemberment, but she was now able to realize that no matter what happens to our physical bodies, we become whole again on the other side. Sofia has acknowledged her pain, honored it and released it.

"They hugged me," she offered when she came out of trance. "And they showed me the love they have for me. I felt their arms around me. How incredible!"

We spoke for a while about how Sofia loved Gretchen and Sigrid, and how they made her feel like they were fairies. She believes they are sprites. Even today, she feels as though they stay near to her like little fairies.

I was looking forward to seeing Sofia on her next visit. I wondered how her connection with her friends would change her outlook on life.

At her next visit, Sofia bounced in with a much lighter step than the time before. "I feel so much brighter. When I look at my daughter now, I can see Gretchen and Sigrid. I feel like I got my friends back. My daughter even acts like them which sounds crazy, but it's funny! They were always doing wild stuff, and we would all get in trouble for it. I loved those times."

Sofia wanted to learn more about what was possible through trance. She wanted to know about her relationship with her husband. "I'm always so jealous, and I don't know why."

I performed a hypnotic induction, and she quickly slipped into a trance state to begin a journey back in time.

"I'm on a large, wooden boat." She tried to figure out what time period she was observing, but she was unable to identify it initially. "The boat reaches a beach and it looks like an early settlement with a row of log cabins. I am a female with dark, curly hair. I am now older with graying hair. I'm in Jamestown. It's a brand new settlement."

I encouraged her to see if she recognized anyone from this time and place.

"I recognize my husband," she observed. "He's my son, and we're not very close. There's coldness between us. I think it's because of his wife. His wife seemed to replace me. I like her, but she can't make him happy. Something is burdening him. I see him on a beach near the town. He is dragging people who have died and bringing them to a boat. He is a gentle soul but so very sad. There's a cloud over him. I love him, but it's painful for me to see him so sad. He carries a lot of pain."

Sofia's time in the past ended, but an epiphany came over her. "I understand my relationship with my mother-in-law now. It's not about me; it's about her son. No one can help him to be happy; he is just not that way. I thought it was because she didn't like me, but now I understand how it feels to be the mother-in-law. I didn't get it before."

Sometimes it takes time for the "Aha!" moment to hit, but when it does, nothing could be more powerful.

"My husband! I felt like his wife took him away from me. I felt like she replaced me. But now I can see that that's how I felt in a past life. It's the same feeling I have today when I feel jealousy. I understand it now. It doesn't have to be this way."

At Sofia's next session, she wanted to share how much better she had been feeling and how much more joyful she was. She also explained that her jealousy with her husband had almost completely vanished. She wanted to focus this session on her life's purpose. I thought it might be time to go into the Akashic Records to find her answers.

"My mom is here," she expressed as she entered the garden, "and she is in a red boat. She is rocking it back and forth. She is telling me to be brave. 'Don't be afraid,' she said."

Sofia had no idea what her mother was talking about, so I suggested that she ask.

"Life. She is saying that I should not be afraid of life. 'Don't be afraid of the journey,' she's explaining. 'Yes, you will have bumps and bruises along the way, but be strong.' I am more relaxed than I have been in a long time, and I feel deeply loved. She was a Buddhist Monk in a different lifetime. She has so much wisdom. I feel divine love. It pours out of her. I have never experienced this from her before because we weren't very close. It feels like I am experiencing a cleansing."

Tears began streaming down her face, and I felt it was time to move on to the Akashic Records. Sofia moved quickly into the Akashic Library as if she had been there before. Many times in our sleep, we investigate the Library but remain unaware of it when we awaken.

"There's no ceiling, and it goes on forever," she explained. "There are no walls either. It's infinite. I have the feeling that I'm floating. I see old, old books, but there is one in particular with a crystal album cover that's mine."

"Put your hand on the book and ask it a question," I suggested.

"What is my life's purpose?" she asked.

As I have explained earlier in a previous story, when you first open your Book of Life, the pages are all blank. That's because you do not read your Book of Life, you experience it.

"My book has a crystal cover," she described. "They are telling me that this is so I wouldn't be afraid of it. I'm curious to see what's inside. The parchment paper is blank, and I feel like I want to write in the book. I hear words being spoken but only in my head," she continued. "They say, 'My gift is the writing and so you shall...'"

There was a brief pause while Sofia made sense of this half-statement.

"I'll write children's books," she explained. "Pages and pages of children's stories."

"I see a baby sprout coming out of the book," Sofia laughed. "It's like I'm in Jack and the Beanstalk. My daughter and I are hanging on it. It keeps growing and I hear someone say, 'Be with the children. Keep them safe. Listen to their stories. See them and re-enact their stories.'" This was interesting because Sofia was a drama teacher in an elementary school before the birth of her daughter.

"We're now in a tree house, and it's magnificent. We're having a tea party and just hanging out. There's a hammock and Annie is having so much fun! I hear another voice say, 'Write stories for children. I'm to write about real people but turn them into real life heroes. Weave in simple household chores and turn the mundane into something magical.'"

The smile on Sofia's face was magical. She looked very peaceful. She was getting peace of mind while in the divine state of mind.

"I hear them again," she continued. "'Stop reliving the negative aspects of your childhood and live your life and enjoy Annie's childhood.'"

Sofia said, "That makes so much sense to me. I just can't believe it. It's so true. I haven't been enjoying her, and I need to do that."

Because Sofia had spent so much time ruminating over her fear of death and the grief that she'd felt from losing her childhood friends, she had not been emotionally available to her daughter. Now she understood that there's so much more to life; so much more is out there and the only thing that matters is love: spreading love, sharing love, and giving love.

At the end of our session, Sofia exclaimed, "Oh my gosh, I just realized - the house - the tree house! I have been pinning pictures of tree houses to Pinterest. And now I'm to use them in my stories! I can't believe that. It's amazing!"

Sofia bounced into her next session with glee. The look on her face had changed so much from when I'd seen her for the first time. I was happy to see the joyful transformation.

"Guess what?" she began. "I told my mother all about our last session, how she immersed me in love! Do you remember it?" She asked.

"Of course," I responded.

"My mom cried, and she thanked me for telling her about it. She seemed to feel really overwhelmed that I finally understood her. I felt she was my nemesis, but I was so wrong. We hugged so tight like it was the first time I'd ever experienced that. It felt so good."

Sofia said that she was now devoting time to writing while Annie takes her naps. She was seeing visions about how to begin her story. Her husband, Richard, would go into the kitchen to get something from the refrigerator, and suddenly...the mundane became magical for Sofia.

Sofia asked if it were possible to see a pet that had died. "I think my dog is my cat reincarnated. Is that possible?"

"Why wouldn't that be possible?" I asked.

Sofia and I decided that perhaps a visit to the meditative garden again under hypnosis would allow her to make contact with her beloved pets. We did the usual induction and I guided her to the garden.

"He's here! I know it's him!" Sofia said, referring to her cat Sebastian. "But he's like a small horse or a donkey. It's weird because he looks different, but I know it's him." She stopped for a moment and the room was silent. Then she giggled, "He's eating out of my hand."

"Can you ask the animal if your dog is a reincarnation of your cat?" I waited as she asked the question.

"I'm right! My dog Sonny is a reincarnation of my cat Sebastian! He is afraid something might fall on him because a bookshelf fell on my cat, Sebastian, and his leg became paralyzed as a result. Sonny walks around looking up most of the time with a frightened look on his face because he remembers how painful it was to be accidentally injured this way. He takes care of my daughter and apparently he wants a can of tuna!" She burst out laughing. "I just bought a can of tuna yesterday. I'll have to give it to him. How funny!"

We both laughed and then Sofia became silent again. I waited for her to tell me what she was experiencing.

"My guide is here asking, 'Remember me?' I'm being led to a picnic area, I guess. There's a man with sandy brown hair who's coming toward me, and he has a candle in his hand. I know him from a previous lifetime. I keep hearing someone say that he was my brother, and he wants to give me love."

Sofia was quiet for a moment. "He's giving me love, and it's flowing toward me and wrapping around me like a white cocoon of light. It's Angelic, and it's just pouring into me."

I let her linger in this love for a while knowing that this was what she needed.

"He says, 'your wish is fulfilled,' but what does that mean?" she wondered aloud. "I'm going to have a burst of life," she said. "Another little girl! And her name will be Samantha, but I'll call her Sam. Oh my gosh, I'll be so old!" She said with another burst of laughter.

Days later, I received a text from Sofia claiming she needed help with sleep. She wanted to see me again, so we scheduled an appointment for the following week. This time Sofia didn't come bouncing cheerfully into my office. Instead, when I greeted her, the first thing I saw was weariness.

Sofia began by describing her daily routine, mostly nursing and caring for her 18-month-old daughter. She explained that her daughter had been sleeping in the same bed as her and her husband since she was six months old. Sofia said that she was practicing Attachment Parenting, but felt that there was too much attachment. Her daughter would wake up at three o'clock in the morning, nurse, and then fall asleep on top of her. She and her husband wanted to eliminate the crib and get a trundle bed in the hopes that Annie would sleep in her own bed.

Reflecting for a moment on the basics of our conscious and subconscious mind, I reminded Sofia that when children are younger than eight or nine, there is no manager in the office. In other words, the critical mind of a child is not fully developed until they reach about ten years of age. In this particular situation, moving her daughter from the warmth and comfort of mommy and daddy's bed to her bed in another room may create a limiting belief within her developing mind. If a thought is connected to an emotion, it becomes a belief. If the belief is not a positive one, it becomes a limiting belief that is stored forever in her subconscious mind. In other words, if Sofia was not careful with the way in which she managed the change for her daughter's sleep arrangement, her daughter may be left with a limiting belief. If she becomes emotional and at the same time has a thought that is completely false like,

'Mommy doesn't love me anymore' or 'I'm not worthy of being in mommy's bed', or worse, 'I'm not lovable,' this limiting belief could enter into her subconscious mind. Of course, these thoughts are false, but her daughter is not able to comprehend the situation at such a young age.

I've seen this happen many times. Parents try their best by reading top selling books on parenting, but they do not consider the possibility that even though infants cannot communicate, they are still able to discern what is happening around them, and they definitely have thoughts about it. I had one client who, during a regression back to his childhood, went back to a time when he was crying and crying for hours in his bassinet. He was emotional and had the thought that no one was there to comfort him. He believed that he wasn't worthy enough for them to stop what they were doing to help him. The emotion and the belief merged to become a limiting belief that kept him from holding onto a relationship. He felt unworthy of having anyone's love which is why he came to see me.

I wasn't exactly sure how to solve Sofia's sleep problem with her daughter still in her bed interrupting her sleep pattern during the night. But then I asked Sofia the following question, and her answer made it clear how I could help her.

"What are you thinking about when you attempt to fall back to sleep?" I asked curiously to see what was going through her mind.

"I worry," she responded.

"About what?" I asked.

"I worry about my daughter. I'm worried about her all the time. I don't leave the house or take her out because I'm so worried," she described. "I'd love to go to the library and have the mommy and me get-togethers, but I don't want to take her out of the house. I'm worried that something will happen to her. I'd love to have fun with her, you know, because she's so young and should be having fun."

Worried parents are a natural phenomenon, but I was wondering where this overwhelming fear was coming from. So, we began the hypnosis session and then I led Sofia to her Akashic Records to find answers.

While she was in a trance state, I suggested to Sofia that if she wanted to, she could always relax in the meditative garden and sleep there. She told me that one night she did just that. She had gone into the healing waters near the garden and fell asleep.

Sofia entered the Akashic Library. "I'm being handed a baby, and I don't know why. It's a boy and I'm holding him." This was the second time Sofia had seen her soon to be born child, only this time it was a boy. "Oh, my gosh. He's mine! Oh God, I'm too exhausted to have another child!" She laughed out loud. "I'm being told that it will be easier this time. I'll have the energy. I won't be so tired. I won't be so worried anymore."

I suggested that she try to find the source of her worry. "Where is the worry coming from?" I asked. Instantly, she moved into a past life.

Smiling, she began. "I'm wearing a gray dress with a little bow on the collar. I'm 13 years old, and I have a brother. He's younger than me, and I feel so much love here with my parents, my brother, and me. We're so happy, and there's so much love and feelings of connectedness between us."

"What's the next significant event in that lifetime," I encouraged.

"I see my old Jewish grandmother. She is just staring at me." Sofia began to cry. "I'm naked now, and I'm with all these other children and we're all naked and cold. We're crying . . . everyone is crying. It's horrible." Sofia was experiencing an abreaction. She began to cry hysterically. I offered to take her above the scene to see it without any emotions, but she wanted to stay within it.

"The children. The children!"

"What's happening to the children?" I asked.

"They're killing the children. They're killing the children! The children! The children!" She was crying uncontrollably now and having a cathartic release. Sofia was reliving her experience and witnessing the murderous deaths of young children during the Holocaust. I brought her to the end of that lifetime, and she immediately became more peaceful. "We were so happy," she began while wiping her eyes. Her mascara was now running down her cheeks. "We had so much love and we lost it all. It was taken from us. I learned that bad things can happen. Trust your inner feelings. If someone is bad, they're bad."

I took her back to the Records suggesting that she leave this scene in the past.

"That lifetime is over now and you no longer have to feel fear about what happened to your family then," I reassured her.

Since our thoughts, feelings, experiences, and beliefs from previous lifetimes are stored in the subconscious mind, sometimes a memory bleeds through into the conscious mind. This creates conflict and turmoil in the current lifetime. In Sofia's case, her fear and worry about her daughter was rooted in a memory from a past lifetime that was torn apart by the Holocaust.

I worked with Sofia to release the memory and heal her inner child. She opened her watery eyes.

"I could see buildings in Germany being totally leveled and then light coming in. Then, I sensed that things were being rebuilt. I can't believe how real it felt. I saw the house and felt the warmth from my family. I felt the love, and when you said to go to the next event I was naked, and people were suffering horribly. It was awful, just awful."

Sofia and I discussed the plain context of this memory. Having been from a past lifetime, she should now be able to release those emotions in order to enjoy the present lifetime with her daughter feeling no fear any longer. I suggested that she would now be able to sleep easier without the worry of a past lifetime subconsciously affecting her thoughts only to keep her awake at night.

"Do you know what's so funny?" Sofia asked. "When my daughter was little, I would look at her and just cry. I didn't know why I was crying, but I'd just cry. It's no accident that I didn't have a child until I was 42! I didn't want to be worried!"

Now realizing how the worry was affecting her, her daughter, and her sleep, Sofia was relieved and looked forward to finally releasing her fear and enjoying this lifetime with her beautiful daughter.

A few months later, Sofia and I spoke. She was sleeping through the night now without any worries or fears. Her daughter was happy to have a new trundle bed in her own room decorated with Disney characters, and Sofia managed to make it a special big girl treat. Sofia was enjoying taking Annie to the children's activities offered all around town, and she laughed when she told me she wanted to have another child. "I'm not exhausted anymore, and I'm really enjoying Annie. Every day we go on another adventure." I was happy to see how relaxed and joyful she was.

Violated and Shamed!

"Just as verbally and physically abused children internalize blame, so do incest victims. However, in incest, the blame is compounded by the shame. The belief that 'it's all my fault' is never more intense than with the incest victim. This belief fosters strong feelings of self-loathing and shame. In addition to having somehow to cope with the actual incest, the victim must now guard against being caught and exposed as a 'dirty, disgusting' person."

~ Susan Forward, Toxic Parents: Overcoming Their Hurtful Legacy and Reclaiming Your Life

Ansar began our session by explaining that he and I were in a similar line of work. He was a Sufi spiritual healer who also teaches Sufism, the Islamic practice of seeking the truth of

Divine love and knowledge through the nature of humanity and God. His goal was to experience and help other people experience the presence of Divine love and wisdom in the world.

"I have been working on myself for a while. It's part of the process to spiritual growth, but I have an issue that I have not been able to face about myself. I've had to deal with it since I was a child."

Ansar's intention was to be free from the childhood trauma and to feel the freedom to be himself fully. He understood the source of his pain, and he felt he could not open up to anyone in his personal life.

"When I was about ten-years-old, I was with my cousin. He was the one who introduced me to sex, and I was not ready for it. I was naive." Ansar paused to take a deeply disheartened breath before he continued. "Basically, I was forced to suck on him, and then he penetrated me. Then he went and told others about the incident, and that put a lot of shame on me that I still carry to this day. I can't get rid of the shame. So I have been given this wonderful gift to perform spiritual healings and do all these wonderful things, but on the inside there is a part of me that's broken. I believe I can overcome it though. It's not just sadness I feel but shame and anger also. The only positive thing about what has happened to me is that I believe this incident is what led me to become a spiritual healer. Now I am hoping to heal myself because I know what happened to me does not define me."

His unrelenting shame nearly cost him his life. "I tried to kill myself. I saw the tunnel, but I came back," his eyes were sullen as he continued. "I still physically feel the pain there in that area. I have felt this pain inside me for over 39 years."

When someone spends as much time meditating as Ansar had, hypnosis comes easily to them. I performed an induction with Ansar, and very quickly he began to see something take shape in his mind's eye.

"I'm in a cave," he started. "There are several different stairwells and statues and carvings on the walls. It's very dark, and I feel lonely. I see reflective water on the cave floor, but the darkness obscures everything else. Looking deeply into the water, I can see my own reflection."

As he looked into the water, Ansar described seeing images of himself as he appeared during different lifetimes. "I see a shimmer of light in the darkness."

"Where do the stairwells lead?" I asked him, but he didn't know. "Take one step at a time," I suggested.

Ansar ascended to the top of the staircase, and he immediately saw an eye. "It's the eye of a child or a baby," he murmured as he clarified his vision. "The eye I see is from a dead baby." He paused for a moment. "I think the dead baby is me. When I asked what knowledge it had for me, it said that it will take me someplace higher, but I don't understand what that means. I feel so sad for that baby and me."

"Why are you being shown this? What does it have to do with you?" I asked as now I was confused.

"Above this place in the distance I see dark clouds and a faint light coming from between the clouds. I feel like it's the light of a fallen angel. It's not, but it feels like that. It feels like separation or a total disconnection from the Source of All Things. Now there's another eye that's opening and looking at me, but it's not human. It opened and then closed right away. It is another being that exists somewhere between Heaven and Earth. It hasn't reached Earth yet. I'm seeing something now, and I believe it's me. I'm being smashed into the clouds because there is no ground there. And it's not fair."

Unclear about what was happening, I needed to understand more, so I suggested, "Ask why you are being shown this?"

"I'm seeing the struggle that I went through as a child. This other being just has it in for me. It's after me and wants to destroy me. It doesn't want me to succeed here in this lifetime. It's like a dragon trying to tear me to pieces and then eat me. It's not a being from the material world. It's not from this dimension, and it's not from the heavenly dimension. It's from somewhere in between."

"Ask how you can stop it," I offered.

"I need to fight back. It's in every fiber of me. It's not of me or part of me, but it's in me. It's merged with me."

"Ask what it needs to separate from you," I began thinking that perhaps I could use parts therapy here.

"I need to suffocate it and purify it from my system by bringing in the light. Now I feel like a part of me is turning and asking for the light. There is a bursting of light and love like a volcano. I have never been here before in any of my meditations. Now I understand why the baby was dead. It was tired, and now it makes sense. The baby was exhausted after going through the trauma. It's terrible; the whole thing is quite difficult. It's the source of all of my problems here, and I need to remove the trauma from me. I see another burst of light, and I realize now that I've felt abandoned by the light. I need to experience what I did as a child."

Ansar took a deep breath as I waited. "Now I feel as though I'm coming into this world or rather, this dimension. I'm descending through the clouds and witnessing all of the trauma." Ansar's face expressed a mixture of indignation, resentment, and humiliation as I knew he was witnessing the worst moment of his childhood. I knew that an inner child healing would allow Ansar to acknowledge and release the pain.

"I understand it now. It has given me compassion for myself and others." It was a new revelation for him, a reframing of a traumatic ordeal. Ansar was quiet for a while as he was absorbing this new information. The he continued, "I feel like it's the beginning of the universe. Light is streaming through the clouds, but there is only darkness and no colors."

His arms and legs twitched, and I asked, "What's happening now, Ansar?"

"I feel like what happened to me when I was ten is like nothing compared to this. This is much more intense. It's so overwhelming. How do I comprehend all of this? I feel like the light can't shine through the clouds. Maybe I don't have enough faith or the belief that the light can pierce through all of this darkness. Inside of me is all this darkness, and the light can't penetrate it. I'm looking for the light. It's fighting the darkness, and suddenly, it's not as dark. But at the same time I feel a pain in my anus, and I'm trying to clear that. It's like a constriction in my anus. I feel tired inside. Not physically, but emotionally. It feels like I'm tired of everything. I feel constriction in my anus whenever I see something that scares me or something I don't like. I don't want to feel my emotions in my anus anymore. It's like experiencing a painful emotion, and all the energy goes to one place in your body. Life was taken out of me. It's like when the baby came to me so lifeless and tired. I was exhausted. I do feel some healing now. It's healing my heart and my body."

It was time to end the session and in closing, I said, "You'll awaken feeling well rested, energized, and healed."

Ansar awoke, and we discussed the session for a few minutes.

"It was like my soul went through this dimension and lost a battle on the way to earth and the entity that won took over my life. It was a strange experience. I feel like life just went in reverse. When I started the trance, I was in a cave with artifacts and statues deep in the ground. Then after that everything became dark and at one point I felt like I was inside a womb, and the baby that came out had just one eye that opened. Then I went back further in time to another dimension where a strange entity made of fleshy scales was beating me down onto a cloud. I could see my soul, and it looked like a vast open space filled with beautiful views. I think the most important thing was feeling the separation from God. I wasn't happy coming to this life, but I didn't realize why or what I had been through."

"When I was young, my brother and my two cousins mocked me so much and caused me to feel such shame that I wanted to commit suicide. I tried to kill myself, and this was the first time I saw the tunnel and the white light."

Children can be so cruel. Bullying can leave the victim feeling a total lack of self-esteem and worthlessness. These feelings can be stored in the subconscious mind and relived over many lifetimes. Having emotions tied to a thought or being shamed into believing falsehoods about ones' self can become a limiting belief. It is limiting because it restricts people from believing in themselves and prevents them from living life confidently, successfully and joyfully.

"Now I realize the entity that was smashing me down was the same entity that caused my cousins to act the way they did toward me. It was trying to break my spirit. But nothing can break my spirit. It's just that my spirit is scared. I admit I have anger about it, but it feels better now understanding why it happened. I know it's not of this life which allows me to release it. I feel much better about things now. Thank you."

All fear and pain are a direct result of feeling separated from our Source. Pain and fear are the ego's delusional perception. It is only an illusion. We have been taught to suppress our painful thoughts, hurts, fears, and emotions. They are difficult to face, so we continue to live with the suffering, sadness, and painful dysfunctions in our lives. Pain and fear are indicators that we have forgotten our soul's awareness. There is only one core fear — the fear of feeling separate from Source. To experience the fullness of life, a person needs first to acknowledge the pain, then honor it by feeling the suppressed pain or fear, and finally surrender it to the highest power, Source.

Once we acknowledge pain and fear by facing it, then feeling it and finally, surrendering it, then and only then can we be filled with love, peace, and joy, and truly experience the fullness of enlightenment.

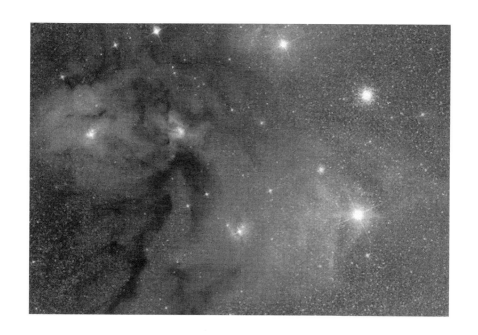

Let It Go

"How can the dead be truly dead when they still live in the souls of those who are left behind?"

~ Carson McCullers, The Heart is a Lonely Hunter

Margo Ann entered my office hoping to understand her present state of mind. "I have anxiety about everything," she stated. "My mom passed nine years ago, and since then I can't feel anything." Margo Ann described herself as being wrought with fear although she did not know the source of her fear. She believed a past life regression might hold some answers for her. Feelings of trepidation kept her from having a restful sleep, and she spent most of the night terrified without any reason known to her.

We began with an induction and a guided meditation then I planned to lead her initially to the garden before moving into a past life regression. However, sometimes things don't necessarily go as planned.

"I can see it. There are multicolored butterflies and a rainbow in the distance. I can see birds, squirrels, and clouds in a beautiful blue sky. A tall man with a long blue satin robe is standing behind a bush, and I can see tiny creatures on the ground. I don't think they were ever in human form. They're watching me, and they're very happy. The tall figure wants me to take his hand. He wants to show me something."

"Go ahead and follow him," I directed her.

"He's taking me up into the clouds and holding my hand as we float up higher. We are just flying through miles and miles of clouds. I sense that he's showing me how much more there is than just earth. Earth is just a fragment of life. I can see land, but I still see beautiful pastures and trees. It's unlike any other world or movie I've ever seen. There's a lot of stress on earth. One day or one second compared to everything else is so unimportant. It's not about the little things here. There's a much greater significance, and it's all connected through experiences that form a greater purpose. It's very important not to stress about insignificant things but instead to focus on our spiritual existence. We need to try to find the spiritual significance of each moment through compassion and kindness. Stress causes us to take our focus off the universal lessons. Whenever we feel empty, sad, or alone, we should think of it as something passing. This is universal. We take from our ordeals what we need to learn about them and then let go because we are so much more than this."

Margo Ann suddenly stopped talking. I had no idea what was happening at this point, but I have learned to allow whatever comes into their experience.

"We stopped flying," she suddenly continued. "Thoughts are being put in my head. We're floating here in the darkness, but there's light coming from within us. There's nothing around us, and everything feels very peaceful. My guide wants me to learn and understand something. He wants me to know that life is about evolving and knowing that there's more than just routine and material success. It doesn't begin or end here on earth. Earth is just one planet in a universe of many planets. If there are people who are stuck, we need to reach out and help them. Maybe if they know there's more, they won't be scared, and they won't give up. Now I see someone else taking my hand. This guide has a velvety purple robe. After I had taken his hand, I began to see a yellow light. I want to see my mom."

Margo Ann had been holding onto her grief for many years, but here she was willing to let go of it to see her mother again.

"I'm being told I would be too scared to see her."

"Sometimes it is easier just to feel their love than to actually see them," I suggested.

Margo Ann started crying. "I'm being hugged. My face and my arms feel numb, but I'm being embraced. A voice tells me that I need to work on shedding my fears, but my mother is here."

"Where does the fear come from?" I asked.

"I wouldn't be able to handle the fear because I'm afraid of dead people."

"People who have died are not really gone. Their energy just changes form," I explained.

"I can see that now. My parents aren't really gone. Our bodies are just costumes. I can't see my mother, but I can feel her, and I know she's happy. I know she's here. I'm asking the guide to take me somewhere else now. I want to keep learning."

I also wanted to continue learning through her experience, but it was time to end the session. When Margo Ann came out of trance, she was in awe. "Now it all makes so much sense to me. It was so beautiful, and I can see there is no death. There is so much more than this existence. I'm not afraid of death anymore. Wow. That was amazing!"

Ringing in the Ears

"Loving the self, to me, begins with never ever criticizing ourselves for anything. Criticism locks us into the very pattern we are trying to change.

Understanding and being gentle with ourselves helps us to move out of it.

Remember, you have been criticizing yourself for years, and it hasn't worked.

Try approving of yourself and see what happens."

~ Louise L. Hay, You Can Heal Your Life

Many people experience an occasional ringing, hissing or buzzing in their ears. Unfortunately, for some people, the ringing in the ears does not go away. This condition is known as tinnitus. According to Louise Hay's renowned book, You Can

Heal Your Life, the probable cause of tinnitus is the stubborn refusal to listen to the Inner Voice.

Millie started our first session with a conversation about her headaches from tinnitus. She had been to many different specialists to try to cure the ringing in her ears, but she was unsuccessful. The ringing continued. The only time she was at peace with it was while she was sleeping. What she disliked most about tinnitus was that she loved to read, and the constant ringing in her ears made reading almost impossible.

Millie felt that throughout her life she had to deal with people who judged her harshly. Her family, her coworkers, and even her therapists seemed to judge her, and although she relayed the stories to me humorously, she experienced the judgment as deeply hurtful. As a comedian, she said that she used their criticism as material for her stand-up routines as well as for the new book that she'd just finished writing.

We invoke laughter as a defense mechanism to guard ourselves against the fear of pain. Being able to laugh at events that have happened in our lives makes the events more tolerable. Looking at a hurtful memory through a prism of humor eases the pain one would expect to feel and helps keep a positive, optimistic view of upsetting situations, disappointments, or loss.

"I am either a work in progress or a piece of work!" Millie joked. "I try not to judge others, but I've dealt with judgment all my life." Millie was very comfortable with her sexual orientation despite receiving negative assessments from others. Her mother and father had been very critical of her, and even her therapist expressed her own views and issues with homosexuality to Millie. But being a lesbian wasn't the crux of her issues. What bothered Millie was judgmental thinking in general.

After discussing her issues for a while, Millie was ready for a hypnotic induction. We began with regression therapy. I guided Millie back to her time in the womb, and she told me that she felt comfortable.

"Mother is in bed, and I can feel her hands touching her stomach. Her belly is big, and she wants to get up, but she's alone. She turns onto her side and struggles to stand and then slips and falls on her stomach. Dad is mad at her for not waiting for him to help her. I'm not hurt, but my mother is very worried."

We progressed to the time of Millie's birth. "Mom's not awake, and I can tell that something's wrong. Mom won't be happy. I have a cleft foot and a hammertoe. She wakes up, and they tell her. She's very upset." Millie was silent for a moment. "'Why can't you be perfect like your brother?' My mom wonders. She's worried about how much money it will cost to fix me. But dad doesn't care about the money. Mom thinks all of this happened because of her fall. She feels guilty about it. She didn't do this, and she shouldn't feel bad about it."

In the spirit world prior to birth into this lifetime, Millie was being shown her mother and father so that she could better understand them. "They look young, healthy and very much alive," she described. "They look like the photos I've seen of them around the time when I was born. I understand their anxiety, and I forgive them. They did a good job and gave me what I needed to be who I am. They love me."

Millie progressed to a time between lifetimes, known as the Conference, where she is being counseled on this lifetime. Various higher-level beings were discussing her spiritual evolution and purpose in the upcoming lifetime.

"I want to do too much," she countered, "I want to do all of this in my lifetime, and they're trying to tell me not to take on so much." Millie began to cry. "Too much. Too much. Too much. I want to finish this and then go back to that place. I wish I could stay here because I love it here so much."

I thought that having a clearer picture of her goals for this lifetime would help Millie make peace with herself. "What are you here to accomplish?" I asked.

"I'm here to be different. It's not an easy life. I'm here to be dropped, not to fit in or make sense, but to love and not judge others. The beings are cautioning me that I'm taking on too much. My mom would always say that I'm too patient, too nice, too emotional, and I wear my heart on my sleeve."

I encouraged Millie to ask the beings about her tinnitus.

"I have too many thoughts and too many directions that I'm trying to take all at the same time. My thoughts are going too fast. They are like the sound of a distant insect flying past my ear. I never stop thinking. I always feel like there isn't enough time. I need to slow down and focus. I'm in a race to the finish because I feel that there isn't enough time." Millie stopped for a moment, and it looked like she was listening to someone.

"I just need to do what's important and say what I came to say to make a difference." Millie was crying now. These thoughts seemed to touch a nerve. "One of them just sent the thought that even if I don't touch one more person, I've done enough."

Millie wanted to know how to release the pain that she felt. "It's up to me. I need to choose. I need to stop judging myself for not doing more. I need to accept that I'm doing enough," Millie cried deep emotional tears. "The voice in my head is telling me to stop doing what I'm doing. It's saying I want to keep going, but I have to stop. I can release it now if I accept that I've done enough, and I stop judging myself. Instead of saying I should have done more by now I need to say I've done enough. I need to stop second guessing myself if I'm going in the right direction."

"The beings are embracing me now, and I'm getting bathed in light. The light is going through me, and it feels like love. I'm forgiving myself. It's a new sensation for me that's really freeing, and I feel much lighter. Why have I been holding onto this weight?" she asked. "They're telling me that it's the weight of having to walk the talk. I'm hiding behind the weight, and I need to stop hiding. I know what to do and I should just do it. It will be easier now because I forgive myself for waiting so long. I've been afraid to do so many things that I feel I should have done sooner. It's not too late for me. I just need to stop judging myself."

Millie's original intention was to stop judging others, but she realized now that judging herself was the bigger issue. Coming to the realization that she had already done enough and needed to do no more was uplifting. It would be up to her now to walk the talk by continuing to acknowledge that she has already made a difference. She had indeed helped enough people pursue their own spiritual journeys. Now it was time for her to start approving of herself to hear and discern more clearly where her own journey would now take her.

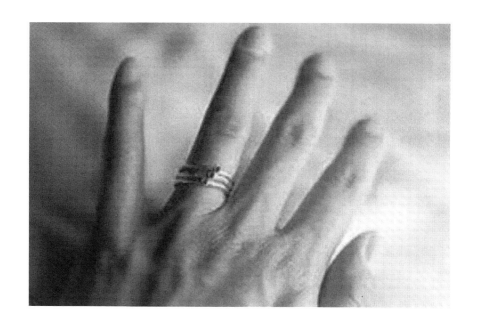

Switching Rings

"When we run, hide and try to deny our trauma the little boy or girl within comes back to seek validation, healing and peace."

~ Cecibel Contreras

Lylah had finished raising her son when she began raising her eight-year-old niece. She was a kind and intelligent woman who successfully stopped smoking years ago after just one session of hypnosis. That was the good news. Today she was in my office for another reason.

"Weight," she started. "I need to lose weight. I quit smoking when I was 30 using hypnosis. I'd began smoking when I was 11, so you have to know that I truly believe in hypnosis."

Lylah was worried that she would not be around to raise her niece if she didn't lose the extra 120 pounds that she was carrying on her little frame. Her feet dangled off the chair unable to reach the floor. She was unable to stick to the gluten-free diet that she'd been following. "I cringe at the word 'diet,'" she continued. "It sounds like 'deprivation' to me. I always prefer using the phrase, "Healthier eating style' because that's easier to maintain than a 'diet' is."

Lylah openly admitted she feared she was keeping the weight on as protection. She was abused at eight years of age and raped at age 14 by her girlfriend's brother. But later we learned during a hypnotic trance, she was also molested at age five.

"I've tried to tell myself that that's not me anymore, but I don't really mean it," Lylah said. "I thought I'd handled the abuse really well because I didn't tell anyone. My parents even got a divorced and I kept it to myself."

Because the critical mind doesn't develop until eight or nine years of age, everything that happens prior is saved in the subconscious mind as the truth. So at an early age, Lylah was told she was a bad girl, and her subconscious mind reminded her of this belief day-after-day especially when she encountered a trigger.

"If I smell his [the boyfriend's] cologne or someone says something to me, or I get too many compliments, I go right back to that time," she explained.

A smell can bring back a flood of memories that can influence people's feelings and moods. This happens because the olfactory bulb, or the nexus of nerves coming from the nose, is located in the brain's limbic system that deals with emotions as well as memories. As I have stated before, when a child experiences an emotion that is tied to a thought, it can become a limiting belief that hides in the subconscious mind. If a smell is also associated with this experience, it surreptitiously interlocks with the memory which can create a powerful response almost instantaneously. In other words, when you smell something new, you automatically link it to an event. This often happens when we are young and encountering smells for the first time. Infants who are exposed to cigarette smoke, alcohol or body odor may react adversely to the same smell later on as adults. Since the smell is a trigger, the mind goes searching for the smell and for the conditioned response that is attached to it. Once it finds the conditioned response such as a mood or feeling it is immediately felt or acted upon.

I began the induction with Lylah and slowly she slipped into a trance. We started by visiting the garden.

"I can see my mother." She immediately began crying.

"I cried for my mother for ten years after she died," Lylah explained. "Now I can see that she didn't die. She's very much alive. I just missed her for all of these years."

Lylah was still crying, yet it seemed she was happy to experience being with her mother again.

"Mom," she started, "are you switching the rings on my fingers at night?" Lylah asked. We hadn't discussed this question during my intake interview, but Lylah now signals that her mother says, "Yes."

"I thought so," Lylah replied. Apparently, Lylah was given her mother's rings. Lylah likes to wear each ring on a different hand. Although occasionally, Lylah awakens after a night's sleep and finds both rings on the same hand which is just how her mother used to wear them.

"I don't know how she does it," Lylah wondered. "I have gained so much weight that I can't even get the rings off myself!" We both laughed.

"She knows I'm going to be OK. She's with me all the time, and she's telling me to lose the weight. She says I need to love myself, and I need to take care of myself before I can take care of other people." She stopped talking to me and spoke out loud to her mother, "That's what I am doing now. I'm taking care of myself before other people."

Lylah began to weep uncontrollably. "She's showing me her love for me by hugging me."

I waited patiently for Lylah to feel the love from her mother.

A few minutes later she whispered, "Mother is leaving now."

Sometimes taking a client on a journey into the future can have profound effects. I chose to future pace Lylah because I wanted her to experience a progression instead of a regression. In a progression, the client experiences future options. I guided her to a bridge that represented the bridge to her future and explained that once she crosses over it, she will be in a future dimension. Here there will be two paths. For Lylah, one path will be continuing to live with the weight while the other path will show her how her life will be without the weight.

"Tell me what you see," I said to Lylah after she was ready to take a look at her future.

"I see myself with Diabetes, and it's hard to walk. I can't keep up with everybody, and I'm very tired. I'm not able to enjoy life. My body is aging prematurely. I can see myself feeling scared of being alone. I'm very lonely and embarrassed because I have a son who is a doctor, and he has a mother who is very unhealthy. I'm raising Shannon, my niece, and I can't take care of her properly. It scares the shit out of me. I ache when I eat." Lylah was able to experience her future as a woman with weight problems, and it wasn't pleasant. She didn't want this to be her future.

"Let's look at the other path," I suggested.

"It's a year later. I have released much of the weight. I've stopped eating gluten, and I'm able to participate in activities with my family. I can exercise again, and I'm happy. It has been three years now, and I am a size 12 which makes me happy."

Next, I wanted to take Lylah back in time to her childhood regression to have a better understanding of the limiting beliefs she was holding on to; the ones which were preventing her from releasing the excess weight that she carried.

"I'm in the house. His house. My brother's friend. We're in his room, and he closes the door. He lifts me up onto the bed, and as I'm sitting there, I realize that I don't want to be there. He's just standing there, staring at me and it scares me. I feel like I did something wrong. The whole situation is strange, and it doesn't feel right. He unzips his pants, and they drop to the floor. He wants me to touch him, but I'm saying no. He says, 'Don't you have a brother?' and I say, 'Yes.' He says, 'Well he has one, but mine is just bigger.' Then he forces me to touch it. He pulls my head closer and forces me to put my mouth around it. I can smell his odor. He's holding my head, and he keeps pushing it into my mouth harder and I'm choking on it. Something came out of it, and I'm choking and gagging now. I can taste him, and I'm appalled by it. I'm so scared and afraid he's going to tell his family about what I did. I felt like I was the one who did something wrong. I'm too scared to tell anyone what I did. I'm so bad. I know I'm going to be in big trouble. I never told anybody."

It was time to heal her inner child. First, I instructed Lylah to tell her younger self, the little girl who had been abused, that it wasn't her fault and that she didn't do anything wrong. Adult Lylah cradled her little inner child and hugged her so tightly that she absorbed her right into herself. Lylah cried and released years of fear, anger, and nightmares. "This makes me so happy," she said through teary eyes.

Lylah and I then took some time to mentally erase the trauma. Lylah took an imaginary eraser and erased the entire scene from her mind.

I wanted her to take some time to heal. I brought her to the healing waters near her meditative garden where she witnessed the toxins floating off of her like paint being spilled from a paint can. She took a brief swim with a dolphin in the healing waters and then returned to her garden. Lylah enjoyed the peaceful garden as she had not felt that much peace in a very long time.

Blocked

"If you hold back on the emotions--if you don't allow yourself to go all the way through them--you can never get to being detached, you're too busy being afraid. You're afraid of the pain, you're afraid of the grief. You're afraid of the vulnerability that loving entails. But by throwing yourself into these emotions, by allowing yourself to dive in, all the way, over your head even, you experience them fully and completely."

~ Mitch Albom, Tuesdays with Morrie

I could see immediately when Amy showed up at my office that she was in emotional pain.

"I'd like to stop smoking, but that's not why I am here," she began. "I know I need to stop smoking, but I've been through too much in my life to worry about that now. Once I decide to quit smoking, I know I can do it but I'm just not ready now. So where do we begin?"

"Okay, let's not worry about smoking, now," I confirmed. "What would you like to focus on to improve your life?"

"I've been through a lot in my lifetime especially in the last three years. I'm a very spiritual person. I can see things in what most people would call dreams, but there's a difference for me between a dream and a revelation. I'm given information in a revelation, and it does help me, but it is almost like I'm my own worst enemy because I'm living in a material world, but I also recognize that there's a huge spiritual energy that I'm working with that's beyond my comprehension."

"Do you see people in your revelations?" I asked because I wanted to know whom she might encounter in her garden.

"Oh my gosh, I have guides, but let me give you a little bit of history. I have always been drawn to knowledge, any kind of knowledge. My husband's major was theology, and he studied at Fordham University. We were Catholics, but we converted to Judaism, not for the religion, but for the sake of becoming well rounded in our spiritual pursuits. I have specific entities that I know are my guides. I smell them, and I feel them. I know them very well. I know when they are speaking to me. They talk to me telepathically. I believe in God, and sometimes I see saints. It's not something that has happened very often, but every now and then I'll see them. I have revelations about things. Sometimes, when I'm sleeping I'll begin to have a revelation, but I'll wake up, and then I'll see the vision in a wakeful state. When I was a child, I thought I was crazy because I would see and hear things. I would go to therapy for it when I was young. When I met my husband, I became more aware because of his knowledge of spiritual things and it just took me to another level. So at this juncture I kind of feel that

I am my own worst enemy because I have to live and function in this material world. And knowing that another world exists, I sometimes long to let go of the material plane so I can just embrace that other place because I know it's there. I struggle a lot with that."

Twice now Amy mentioned being her "own worst enemy." I took note of this because there may have been something symbolic in that phrase.

"So, let me summarize what I'm hearing you say," I began. "You want to let go of materialism to embrace spiritualism."

"Yes, exactly. I feel like lately my spiritual development has been blocked. I meditate daily, but recently it has not been flowing as it usually does because I have a lot of additional responsibilities that I didn't have before. I have worldly responsibilities. They hinder me, and I don't like that. I don't feel grounded, and I don't feel centered. I don't see adversity as bad. I've learned that if you have adversity it's just a part of the process that takes you to another level. It's not because you are bad or did something wrong. It's just part of the process of understanding the universe better. I feel like I'm in this gray, blurry place right now, but I know where I should be and where I want to be. It is just getting there that's the problem."

"Explain this 'material' thing to me," I asked as I wanted a better understanding of her dilemma.

"Just worldly worries about money, the kids, normal stuff. But I know deep down that everything will work itself out. It's my truth but then sometimes I vacillate between spiritual truths and material truths and that just perpetuates the struggle."

"Describe the struggle," I prompted.

"I've suffered losses, like, for example, three years ago my husband passed. Forty-five days later my mom passed. Thirty days later my stepson committed suicide. A year later my 20-year-old was diagnosed with complete kidney failure. It's just been a lot of stuff." Amy began tearing up. "I'm not crying because I'm sad; I'm crying because I know it's a part of my process, and I'm trying to embrace that and be at peace with it. It's hard and what keeps me going is my relationship with my guides and with God and my spiritual self. That really keeps me centered. I haven't skipped a beat, you know, my husband passed and like I said I realized that nobody belongs to anybody. The people we love have a beginning, middle, and an end. Obviously that was my husband's end here on the material plane, and I'm okay with that, but I struggle with him being gone. I know this is kind of like a paradox, but I know he is with me more now than he was when he had a material form. He can be with me now all the time whereas before we couldn't always be together physically. He's everywhere. He does come to me, and I journal every day about him. I've done that since I was young and that kind of helps me see where I've been, where I'm at, and where I'm going. When my guides come to me, or the spirit of my husband visits, I just journal and sometimes it doesn't make sense at the time. But then later I'm like, 'Oh my God,' and I go back and read it and it makes sense to me. But lately, I don't know. I'm at a big question mark. I don't know. I believe in medicine, but I don't take any medications. I take care of my medical issues homeopathically and with herbs. I make my own oils and basically that has kept me sane."

"Don't you think it's strange that you are so committed to a homeopathic regime, but you still smoke?" I just had to ask. It was such a paradox.

Amy was shocked that I paired these two things together. She hadn't thought of it that way before. We talked briefly about past life regressions, and she said, "I've never felt like my smoking belonged to me. Perhaps, it's something I do because of a past incarnation."

"I feel like I'm at a point in my life where I'm truly ready to let go of the losses. I'm ready to move forward by getting rid of the losses, whether it is conscious or subconscious. I feel like there is guilt simply because you are living. You are surviving. My husband was my soul-mate, and I was very blessed in this lifetime to have had him with me. I know I've been with him before. When I first met him, I said I've known you. I've known you my whole life. And I'd just met him. So that bond, though I feel like I've lost it, I know that I haven't. I just feel right now like I am blocked."

We discussed the idea of going into a hypnotic trance and Amy explained how she has slipped into past life experiences before. While she was talking to her mother in a conscious state, she watched her mother morph into a queen dressed in a black velvety dress. She could see herself being led to a guillotine. "My mother had me executed in that lifetime." Despite this, Amy didn't have any hatred towards her mother. However, she found it amusing that at home, whenever she would flip her hair over to dry it, she would feel fear rising inside her.

Amy and I decided that it was time to induce a trance and see what emerged from it to help her deal with the feeling of spiritual disconnection that was burdening her. We began with a regression.

Amy saw herself dressed in 1960s clothing, and she was wearing thick glasses. She was chain-smoking Pall Mall cigarettes the ones with no filters. She was wearing bright red lipstick. "I feel like I smoke because of the spiritual aspects of smoking and not for material reasons. I actually don't like smoking."

Amy then saw herself floating above her body at night. "That's scary," she said. "I don't like that."

"You're experiencing astral projection," I explained. "Many people are able to separate their astral body from the physical body. At night, the astral body leaves one's physical body, and travels while their physical body stays asleep. It is also called an out-of-body experience."

Next Amy saw a prism of light all around her. "It feels loving," she said. "Like God is all around me. I feel something like a strobe or a heartbeat, and I smell roses."

"God's energy is good energy. It's love. Do you sense your body?" I asked.

"I sense a block. I can't get past the block. It's not something tangible that I can look at. I can't seem to get close to it."

"Let's communicate with the block, then," I suggested. "Ask the block if it will communicate with you. Why is it blocking you?"

"It's pain," she said. "It's blocking the pain? 'I am the pain. I'm blocking me.' It says."

"Let's go into the pain. The only way to release the pain is to go into it," I told her.

"I don't want to go."

"Yes, I know, but you want to be unblocked."

"Yes."

"Then we need to go into the pain. You're safe here with me. Go ahead and feel the pain. Go into the pain."

Amy was crying now. "I'm feeling sad. I feel anger and heat, and I see the colors orange and red. I keep fighting it that's the problem."

"Go into it and feel it. If you want to be unblocked, you have to feel it," I repeated.

"I feel angry at God. I'm angry at God, and that's the struggle I have because I know what I know. But a part of me . . . Now I feel my heart (shaking and holding her heart) is warm in a good way right now. I can feel it, but I just want to tell God how angry I am. I'm so angry, but I haven't allowed myself to feel the anger because I don't want God to be disappointed with me."

"He's not going to be angry with you. He wants you to tell him how you feel," I encouraged.

"I'm sorry God, but I am angry. I'm sorry God because of everything that's happened. I'm so angry." Amy was crying uncontrollably now. "I'm on fire; I'm so angry," she wept.

"Be on fire and feel the pain," I urged knowing this would release her block.

"I just want . . . I just want . . . I'm sorry God if I've done something that's caused this. I didn't mean to . . . I didn't mean to . . . (sobbing), and I was angry 'cause of all these things that happened to me. And I fight with myself, and I hold it back 'cause I don't want you to be angry with me. I held back my anger. I held it back!"

"Don't hold it back now. Tell him how you feel," I coaxed.

"And that's the block. That's the block. My love has been taken from me. My love and everything that I was, everything that I came from, the love that I had is gone. And God you took that from me. Forgive me for feeling so much anger."

"Allow it to all come out," I continued urging.

"I don't want to because that means that I am wrong. I want God to know how angry I am that everything was taken from me. I'm so angry. I am sooo angry. I feel lost and betrayed and scared. I feel the anger as heat."

"Ask him to take the pain from you," I suggested. "Tell God that you surrender the pain and anger to him."

"I do," she said.

"Ask him to take the pain," I repeated.

"Please take this from me so I can continue to do the work you want me to do," Amy said. "To continue to be the person I need to be. I don't want to struggle anymore. I don't want to live a lie. I try to suppress the anger because I don't want you to be angry with me. But it's there. I keep stuffing it and stuffing it further and further into myself because I didn't want to say that I was angry at you God because everything you do is for me, even the bad stuff. I know that. And that's what I've been fighting. But I am angry. I am. And I can't change that, and now I don't want to change that. But I want to move past that anger. I feel like, why me? Why did I have to lose my love? Why?" Amy took a long, deep breath.

"Surrender the anger, the hurt, and the disappointment," I said offering her a suggestion.

"Please take this from me," she pleaded, and we waited. "The light is changing from red to yellow. It's getting cooler, and my heart is slowing down. The light is iridescent now and beautiful." Her countenance lightened.

"I'd like to take you to the healing waters," I told her. "Do you see a body of water?" I asked fully expecting a positive answer. Then I explained how the healing waters work.

"Yes," she said and continued, "The water is turquoise, and I see turquoise coming off my feet."

Amy was able to see the negative energy leaving her body through the healing waters. The energy looks like paint that has been spilled in the water that slowly floats away and disappears.

"I see blackness coming off my chest."

"Is it tar from the cigarettes?" I asked. "Perhaps your body is releasing and cleansing itself of any toxins and poisonous thoughts." I added this suggestion as a precursor for her to quit smoking.

"I love the water. It relaxes me," Amy continued, "I love anything that has to do with water. Water makes me feel calm and peaceful. I feel so much love. I can feel my heart fill with light. It's so peaceful and so good. I've been struggling for so long, and I've been worried for so long."

"Is the block gone now?" I asked.

"I was afraid to feel it. But everything just stopped, and now I feel like I can move forward. I just miss my husband. I miss him so much."

"It's time to leave the healing water and go back into the garden. One. . . Two. . . Three. Be there!"

"I'm in the garden, and I see him. He's there! I can feel him and smell him. He's telling me that he loves me more than anyone else. (Long pause) I didn't understand that. But now I do. He lost me before in another lifetime, but he found me again in this lifetime. And when you lose something and finally find it, you never want to let it go. So you hold on to it again, so you don't ever lose it again." Tears appeared again in Amy's eyes.

"He wants me to know that he's always with me." Then she added, "And that I'm not living what I've learned. I haven't done anything wrong. It was just his time to go. I can't hold on like this anymore." She whispered as if she was speaking directly to him, "I know I have to let go." It was clear she hadn't done that yet. "He wants me to love my children just like he loved me. He tells me that he knows that I know how to give and receive that love, but now I have to let go. He says, 'Don't be afraid anymore and don't be angry anymore because he's always there with me.' He said that he saw me the day after he died. He saw me crying over him. I said get up, get up, get up. He's always smiling, and it's okay not to worry and just to live. But I haven't been living. And all I do is worry about whether or not everyone is okay. And meanwhile, I'm not okay. You need to be okay first, and then everyone else will be okay . . . I smell roses again," she said taking a deep breath in as though she smelled them.

"He has to go," she announced. "He doesn't want me to hold onto him anymore because it's hurting me. That's why I feel anger. He says I'm not allowing myself to do what I need to do. He says he's always there. Always."

Amy became silent for a moment, and I waited. And then finally, she said, "Now I see a pinkish-golden light coming from above me shining down. My husband says it's time to let go of his hand. I can feel him moving forward, and I can breathe in his love and his energy, and I don't need to hold his hand anymore. He's going to help me feel him differently. He says it's time, and I'm letting him go. I don't want to, but he says he's not a physical being anymore. I smell him, and I feel his love and he says that's how I'll know that he's there."

It was time to bring Amy back to a conscious state. Her breathing was calmer, and I felt as though she had released the block that was holding her back. She had closure with her husband who had clearly indicated that it was time for her to move on. Feeling angry with God is a normal human

182

experience but suppressing the anger only leads to pain and eventually illness. When Amy harbored her feelings of anger toward God, she felt guilty, disconnected, and alone. By allowing her to experience the pain, she was able to move through her feelings and then move on. It was a critical step to removing the blocks.

Just as I readied to conclude my session with Amy, something unexpected happened.

"I don't know what's here," she said. "I feel something heavy on top of me like a weight."

"Okay," I said, "let's find out what it is. Ask if the heaviness will communicate with you?"

Amy's voice became deeper. "It's not happy," she said, breathing more deeply now. She kicked the footstool away and sat straight up in her chair. "It's not happy," she repeated in an even deeper voice. "It's angry because it doesn't want this to happen." Her voice became louder, and she repeated the statement again. "It doesn't want this to happen."

I reminded Amy that she was safe and encouraged her to ask the heaviness what it wanted. "What is it doing here?" I asked. Amy inhaled deeply and then gasped as I continued to speak. "Bring the light in. Let the light come in. Surround yourself with the light."

She took another deep breath and then spoke in a different voice, "I've have been here for many, many, many, many lifetimes and I don't like this."

"Thank it for whatever lessons you've learned," I began, "but tell the heaviness it is time for it to leave. It's time to leave."

"That's the thing," Amy explained, "that's the thing. It's not 'it.' It has nothing anymore, and it knows that. Now God is putting his sword down, and He's very powerful. I see the Archangel Michael coming, and he is putting his sword (she holds up two hands as if she is holding a large sword, and she slices it in half and then again in a horizontal slash) and he's cutting and he's breaking and It did not want this to end. It knows it's over . . ." She told me pausing momentarily. "I see the light of the Lord in his magnificence, and I'm humbled by it. The power of this energy is of God, of Jesus and the Holy Spirit. Whatever this thing is, it's angry, and the power of God doesn't matter. This is what's been fueling my anger, despair, and depression.

"Is it gone?" I questioned knowing it was just negative energy.

"It will be. It will be," Amy said as she moaned and then began praying out loud while holding one arm up and the other as though she were holding an imaginary scale. "It's the Lady of Justice. I wear a blindfold because there is no justice except God's justice. God's Will will be done. I see a group of nuns in a circle, and they're singing and the light is coming from above into the middle of the circle. This blackness is in the middle of this circle. The scales of justice are balanced. It's done. The light will remove this darkness. It's so beautiful. The choir and the music and the sounds are so beautiful. I don't feel any of the pain anymore. My heart just feels so much joy. It doesn't matter anymore. I feel like the weight has been lifted off me, and I can feel my heart again. My eyes feel like they're swollen."

"Are you ready to come back?" I asked.

"Yes."

I brought her back to a waking state.

"The light and the energy here is totally different from when I first walked in. I feel like I'm in a different place," she remarked as she looked around the room astonished.

I asked her if she remembered the session.

"I remember smelling roses, and I remember seeing my husband," she offered as she came back to full consciousness.

"Do you remember what he said to you?"

"No. But I remember a feeling of heat and then a feeling of cold. I feel like a totally different person! When I got here, I was filled with anxiety, and now I feel totally different and relaxed."

I promised to send her the audio recording of this session.

"I told you when I started that I felt blocked, but now I feel that the block is gone. I'm embarrassed that I don't remember."

"I recorded it for you so you can listen to it later," I said. "How long do you think you were in a trance?"

"A few minutes," she answered.

"Actually, you were in a hypnotized state for over an hour," I explained. "You'll see that your block is gone."

"You know it's funny, but I just thought to myself, do I want a cigarette? But I feel like I don't want one, and that never happens. Thank you," she said. "I would like to come back."

"Anytime," I smiled.

We have been taught over the years to suppress our pain. It begins when we are very young, and we are told, "It's OK, don't cry." As we age, we are told, "Don't think about that," or "Stop worrying, everything will be fine." It is worse for men, as they are told, "Real men don't cry." Yet suppressing our emotions keeps us from experiencing real joy. By stuffing our painful emotions deep inside, we eventually try to numb the unhealed pain or fear by developing unhealthy habits. Habits such as smoking, drinking, overeating, irresponsible spending, acting aggressively, manipulating others, compulsive worrying, negative thinking, judgmental speech, criticism, anger, guilt, stress and chronic lying are behaviors that develop due to harboring suppressed unhealed pain and fear. They are indicators warning that something needs to be faced, felt, acknowledged, and released.

Amy's deep emotional outcry (her release of her anger towards God) was the expressed outcome of the HOPE Technique©. 'Healing Our Painful Emotions' is a tool given from Jesus for effective emotional healing.

I Love Myself Now

I try not to live my life worrying about what others think.

A core spiritual quality is non-judgment, which is not just about not judging others,

but also not living your life worried about others judging you.

~ Deepak Chopra

When Ally came in, I could see years of abuse, self-judgment and exhaustion in her eyes. "I've had a traumatic upbringing. Horrible. My mother was an alcoholic, and she has been abusive to me for as long as I can remember. I remember being in the crib at two years old, looking up at her screaming at me, and I had no idea why! I just remember her screaming and thinking, what have I done? I knew from a very young age that my mother didn't want me. My dad told me years later about this soft spot on my head. "Here," she said, "feel it." Ally bent her head down, flipped her sparse blond hair to the side and showed me a quarter-sized soft spot in her head. "Here is an injury from when my mother tried to abort me with a coat hanger. My dad told me about it. She didn't want me."

Ally's deep pain was holding onto her tightly, and I could see why as she continued.

"I tried to commit suicide at 12 years old and then again several more times, but I didn't succeed at any of those attempts. I'm much better now because I'm getting past the grief of losing my family. My sister died at age 46 of lung cancer. A year later my brother died of lymphoma at age 30. Three years later my dad died of prostate cancer and six months later my mom died of a heart attack. Two weeks after that my other brother died of a drug overdose. Needless to say, I nearly lost my mind."

I was surprised she was still a smoker after losing so many family members to cancer. Her parents had separated when she was three months old and when I asked her to tell me what it was like living with her mother, she said, "It was like living in hell."

Ally continued to explain her relationship with her mother to me. "I've forgiven her because she was raised without a mother herself. She didn't know how to be a mother. So there was a lot for me to forgive. I forgave her when she died. She was an alcoholic and a drug addict. There was a lot of verbal abuse and fighting in our family. The abuse wasn't just from my mother but also from my brother and sister as well. And everyone in my family including myself was a drug addict and alcoholic. I was a pothead, but I gave up marijuana three years ago. I went to rehab, and the change in me was tremendous. I was either going to die from my bad habits or make big changes in my life. And since I hadn't been successful with my suicide attempts, I had to try to change other things. Once you go to rehab you kind of got to get your shit together, and thank God, I did. So I'm ready to go further and try to heal from within. I didn't work on my childhood while I was in rehab. I blocked a lot of it. I know that. I remember a few things but not many."

We started with an induction and then I led her into the garden. "I just feel very peaceful. I think my mother is here," Ally began calmly.

"What does the garden look like?" I asked trying to gauge the depth of her state.

"Very vibrant colors. Like I've never seen before. I see a golden butterfly that's so peaceful and beautiful."

Once my clients mention butterflies, it is a certainty that they are in a very workable theta trance state. "Is there anything you would like to tell me about the garden?"

"My mother is here, and she's smiling. She's putting her arms around me and crying. She just keeps apologizing to me. She says she did her best with what she knew while she was raising me, and if she could do everything all over again, she would make different choices. Now she's going away." Ally added, "She's gone now."

Ally continued unprompted. "My sister is here too, and she says she's always with me, and she's never left me. I see the whole family together, and they're happy. They want me to be happy too. Jesus is here, and He just said to me to ask for a healing and that it would be given to me."

"Go ahead and ask for a healing," I guided.

"I see the light, and it's peaceful. There are spirits all around and bright orbs. I see a deer and angels and my spirit guide. They are saying they're proud of me because I haven't wavered once from the beginning. God will provide me with everything that I need. 'Go forth on this journey.' Jesus says."

"The Archangel Michael is here too," Ally continued with a look of total peacefulness on her face. "The love of God surrounds me and protects me. The Archangel Metatron is here too, and he tells me to trust myself. Sparkles are everywhere. The whole landscape is glistening."

Ally explored in the garden for some time and then said, "Somebody wants to contact me. Here, nothing is frightening. Nothing is wrong. I don't see who it is or what it is. I'm confused. I don't know who it is. They're not showing themselves to me."

"Ask who it is," I suggested.

"It's a dancing bear of light: a creature that's very childlike, happy, and peaceful. It is the baby I aborted. It's telling me to release the pain. That baby was never meant to be. I'm supposed to release the pain." Ally wept quietly. "I feel so sorry. I didn't know. I feel pain in my heart, and I need to let it go and give it to God. I'm just filled with sadness. My guide is telling me that I have the baby with me now in this lifetime. It is Jessica, my daughter. The baby was reborn as my daughter. It's okay. I feel better. Lighter. The angels are saying that they are always with me. I've never been alone, and I have not been abandoned. I feel peaceful and calm. Jesus is smiling, and he has his hands open and he says, 'For you, my child,' and I see light coming from his hands and going into my heart. I see a lot of light going into my heart, peace and a lot of love. Jesus is telling me that everything is okay. Everything is good. Everything happens in its own time. For me, it's time to heal. I am in the garden, and everything is very tranquil. My brother Ed is just a kid running around in circles. My older brother is with me giggling and looking at me with contentment. He's very happy. I see my Higher Self telling me that there are avenues to every journey and in order to enter the avenues the timing has to be right. And the timing is right. But to do what? I don't understand. The time is now. It's time for growth and healing. It's time to let go of old belief systems." Ally was quiet again for a bit and then she added, "Nothing is happening now. I just feel love and everything is still."

It was time for her to come out of the trance.

"Wow. That was amazing," Ally said as she regained a normal state of consciousness. "I can't believe that I saw my mom! She left rather quickly, but I felt like she needed to go. She needed to heal herself and forgive herself."

Ally explained that she had gotten pregnant three times. "I had three abortions, but I never speak about them. I was in my mid-twenties and a single parent, and I remember the fear of bringing a child into this world when I didn't know what I was doing. So I had an abortion and got pregnant again and again. Two more times after that and now I realize that each time it was the same baby coming back until my second child, Jessica was born. Each time it knew that it was going to be aborted, but being aborted was part of the experiences that it needed to have." Ally stopped for a minute, and I could see she was still processing what she had just experienced. Then she continued, "It was her soul's choice. It was all part of her karma. I'm shivering inside just thinking about it because that's painful stuff. I'm a good person in my heart, and so it killed me. But now I can see that I didn't take its life. I didn't kill it. I gave it life. Wow. I can't believe that." Ally was suddenly overcome with tears, and as she wept, she released years and years of guilt.

This happens often. A client will come out of the trance garden and suddenly like an open spigot, the mind is flushed with comprehension. These are "Aha!" moments that are filled with healing. Once a deep inner emotion is revealed and carefully examined with total understanding and compassion coming forth, then miracles can occur like the miracle of Inner Peace.

"Wow!" Ally said. "I can't believe that for years I thought it was the opposite. How deep is that? You know I'm Catholic, and it is a mortal sin to have an abortion. That's a heavy burden. I guess this was what needed to come out. I feel so content. I love myself now, and I've never felt this way before. It's amazing."

Shortly after our session, Ally trained to be a quantum-healing practitioner, and she is traveling around the country using her talents performing group regressions.

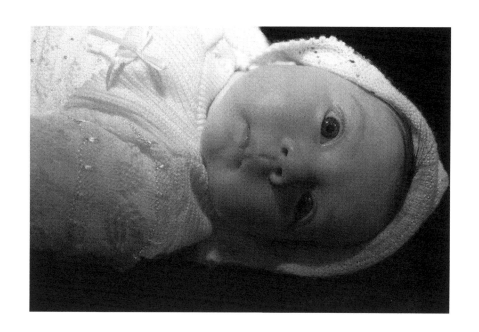

I Ruined Your Life?

"We may feel good about our words, our intentions, and our motivations may be pure, but our message will probably be lost or misunderstood if we overlook how others are going to perceive what we say."

~ Robert E. Fisher, Quick to Listen, Slow to Speak

Despite the fact that good intentions are sometimes misunderstood, they can also be misinterpreted with precarious results. This was the situation with my next client, an early 30-year-old woman who wanted to have a past life regression to understand her dysfunctional relationship with her mother.

"It has to be from a past life," Leena began, "because I never liked her. I've always been angry with her for the way she talked to me and the way she treated my sisters. It was like she didn't want us." She continued, "I think it's because of her that I'm afraid of commitment. Every relationship I'm in lasts only three years . . . to the day!" She added.

"How many relationships have you had that ended exactly three years after they began?" I questioned.

"Three."

"So you've had three relationships that each ended exactly three years after they began. Is that right?" I clarified.

"That's right. And also, when my mother calls me and asks how I'm doing, I resent it. I feel like I'm being forced to talk to her."

I felt that childhood regression therapy would give us some insight into Leena's problems. We did an induction, and Leena began her hypnotic experience in the garden.

"My Grandfather is here," she said. "He's wearing a red and white striped shirt and glasses. It's so good to see his face again. I was beginning to forget what he looked like. He takes my hands. His hands were always calloused and rough from working outside. He always said that I have little hands. He's saying it again to me. He is saying, 'Don't be sad. Everything will be fine and just have faith.' He is always with me. Watching me. I missed him so much," Leena said with tears rolling down her face.

I love when grandparents enter the scene during a regression. Often there is a warm and welcoming feeling, and they can explain things without any emotional issues. It's very healing for my clients.

Leena wept quietly for a few minutes and then suddenly, she spoke again with surprise, "I have black hair. It's really weird because it's cut with an Egyptian style. I have on an Egyptian type of robe and dress too."

I was curious, so I asked Leena to tell me where she was.

"My grandfather is telling me that I am like my mother and the thought of that makes me angry. I don't want to be anything like her. Why do I have black hair?" Leena asked her grandfather. "'You were an Egyptian princess,' he told me."

"Ask him if that is where the relationship issues with your mother began," I prompted.

"'No,' he said. My feelings toward my mother don't come from a past life. He says I need to forgive her because she's done the best that she could."

I thought it would be a good idea to ask Leena's mother to come into the garden.

"My mother is here," Leena announced as her brows furrowed. "And she's crying. She says she always loved me, and she's sorry if she hurt me. Why did you make me feel like your life was ruined because of me?" Leena asked.

Leena explained that she'd made it difficult for her mother. After Leena's sisters had been old enough and she'd left Leena's father, her mother never wanted to bring another man into Leena's life. "'I had three little girls, and I didn't want anyone to hurt you. And I wanted a better life for you,' Mother said."

Leena's mother had had good intentions, but her choice of words had inadvertently crushed her daughter's self-esteem. She would always tell her daughters to get good grades in school, go to college, and get a good job, so you don't have to depend on anyone else. But her mother also counseled her daughters not to get pregnant because "it will ruin your life."

It was the "ruin your life" part of her speech that destroyed Leena's feelings about herself. Of course Leena had interpreted her mother's words to mean 'I ruined my mother's life.' Leena grew up with this belief and seeing her mother angry and upset all the time confirmed this belief. It was probably understood while Leena was still in the womb.

When Leena realized that her mother loved her very much and remained single for fear of a man hurting her children, she understood that her mother was just trying to protect them. Leena was then able to begin to forgive her mother.

"It's raining now," Leena continued. "But Grandfather has an umbrella, and I'm telling my mom that I forgive her. She's leaving now."

Since the issue with her mother had nothing to do with the past, I decided to see what the future might have in store for Leena, a progression. We asked Leena's grandfather to take her to a happy time in the future.

"I see a baby girl. She's in my arms, and I'm holding her. She's so little, and she's wearing a polka-dotted pink hat and little pink dress. I'm so happy. I have long blond hair again. I'm in the baby's nursery and it's all white with two cribs: one that's white and one that's brown. There's another little baby boy in the brown crib. He's older, and he's wearing little jean overalls. He's bouncing in his crib."

I asked if there was anyone else around.

"Yes, my husband is here. He is tall, tan and muscular. He has a beautiful smile with straight white teeth. He has black hair and dark eyebrows. His name is Eric I think. He's kind and gentle."

"How long have you two been together?" I asked. I wanted to know if they'd been together longer than three years.

"Seven years," she laughed. "We were together for two years before we got married. We've been married for five years."

"I guess your three-year jinx is over," I wanted to confirm this for her in her subconscious mind.

"Yes, it is. My mother just came into the bedroom," Leena started, "and she looks so happy. She likes my husband because he's gentle and kind to me. She's picking up her grandson. I'm so glad that she's helping me with my children. I get it now. I didn't get it then, but I get it now. She just wanted the best for us. It wasn't the way she wanted to do it, but she was happy to have us."

Now feeling the love from her mother, Leena was able to fully comprehend her mother's good intentions for her three daughters. It seems that in the future, Leena and her mom will be joyfully raising the little babies together. What could be better than that?

"My grandfather is sitting in the rocking chair. He's watching us and smiling. He still has on his red and white striped shirt and his glasses. He's enjoying the view," she said as a gentle smile lingered on her face.

I Speak to Jesus

"I, Jesus Christ, am not anything or anyone you may think I am.

All I am is love, compassion and non-judgment.

I am God's energy filled with nothing but

love, compassion and non-judgement.

That is all there is of any relevance about who and what I am.

Nothing else matters.

None of the stories you have heard, believe or do not believe,

judge as accurate or inaccurate, matter not one bit.

The only thing that is important to know about who I am is that

I am nothing but love, compassion and non-judgment.

~Jesus"

~ Connie Fox, The Power of You: The End of Pain, Separation, and Fear

Some people can communicate directly with the spiritual realm. Ester Hicks speaks to a collaborative group of entities known as Abraham, John Edward communicates with loved ones who have crossed over, Theresa Caputo conveys messages from the other side, April Crawford speaks to Veronica, Neale Donald Walsh has conversations with God, and of course the recently departed Silvia Brown shared wisdom from the other side for decades.

Connie Fox speaks to Jesus. She is the author of The Power of You: The End of Pain, Separation, & Fear and Help from Heaven. She shares her conversations and wisdom from him in her books. I've read both of her books and loved them, so I was happy to have the opportunity to work with her. (Note: Connie Fox has given me permission to use her real name.)

"You say you communicate with Jesus?" I questioned.

"Yes, for years now," she answered.

"How do you communicate with him? Do you see him?" I wanted to know if she goes into a trance state to communicate with him.

"No. I don't see him, and it's not a voice that I hear in my head. The words just come to me. I hear words with a lot of love and compassion." She continued, "I didn't start to really communicate with him on a heart to heart level until I recently wanted to make conscious contact with God as I began to understand him. I describe it all in my next book, Messages From Heaven: A New Life On Earth."

When Connie first started communicating with Jesus, he told her she would be writing many books. I assumed they would be similar to Neale Donald Walsh's trilogy, Conversations with God. She's already published two books that are compilations of the transcripts of her conversations with Jesus and is presently finishing her third book.

"What would you like to accomplish here today?" I asked.

"I heard you have taken people into the garden to meet their loved ones. I thought, well I was wondering if I could meet Jesus in the garden."

Since Connie already communicates with Jesus, I was fairly confident she would have a magnificent experience and was excited to get started right away. "What are you experiencing?" I asked as she entered the garden.

"It is so beautiful and peaceful," Connie began. "There's freedom here from this horrible world. From the sickness and horribleness, pain and suffering and I feel like this is what I felt before I was born."

No one ever described the garden quite like that before, but I liked it. "Yes, it is. This is what it was like. What else are you experiencing?" I wanted to hear more.

"Lightness. Lightness against the heaviness," Connie looked so serene.

I wanted to move her forward, so I offered, "Sometimes little creatures come to visit in the garden. Friendly little things. Do you see any?" Hypnosis is focused concentration; the more focused someone is, the deeper into a trance they go.

"Yes, I see some bunnies." Connie describes the rest of the garden in great detail as I knew she would.

"What else do you see in your garden? Any entities? What do you sense?" I asked.

"I can't even describe how I feel. I feel like there is someone or something in the background. I can't see them. I can sense someone further in the back. I just don't know where they are." Under Connie's lids, her eyes were busy searching.

"Bring their energy closer. It sometimes takes them a little time to pull their energies together," I suggested.

"Yeah, I feel there's a presence or a beam of light in the background, but I can't see what's there. I can just sense something. I can sense them there. I don't know. It's a God energy," Connie reported sounding a bit confused.

"It's what?" I asked as Connie was so deep in a trance she began to whisper as if she was speaking to someone inside the garden.

"It's God's energy. It's not a--it's just a God energy. It's just like light and energy presence. It's like our Source."

"What does the Source want you to know?" I asked.

"It wants me to know that I'm okay where I am, and I don't have to get somewhere. I can feel content where I am. It's not about getting somewhere in the future, or being in a certain place that's better. I feel like it's wonderful. It's just a presence, and there's no form. It's saying that there's no one place to be coming to."

"Pardon me?" I asked as she was whispering again.

"It wants me to know that there's no place to keep reaching for, but that the place is right there inside all of us. People keep thinking we have to go and reach further or accomplish something more. It's always there, right there. It's right there. I feel like it's pulling, pulling out invisible atoms from my body. Am I able to talk to this energy like that? The energy just continues to pull all these little atoms that are inside my body to it, and they just disappear into it."

I had no idea what was happening, so I allowed some time to pass then asked, "What are you experiencing now?"

"Mmm-mm. I feel like I'm one with Him and no longer separate," Connie's expression was priceless. I could see her expression was one of tranquility.

"You are one with it. Pure energy, just like you are because you're a part of that, the oneness of it all. We all are," I confirmed.

"Yes," Connie smiled.

"Are you ready to move on?" I asked.

"Yeah."

"Thank the energy for coming."

"Hmm-mm, right."

"If you notice in your garden there's a little stream, and over the stream is a bridge. Do you see the bridge?"

"A stream and a bridge. Yeah, I can see it."

"We're going to go over the bridge into another dimension. Are you ready?"

"Hmm-mm."

"There's going to be a beautiful field of gorgeous flowers and colors and rolling hills. On the count of three, you're there. One, stepping onto the bridge, two, stepping over the bridge, three, the other side of the rolling hills, see the beautiful fields. Do you see them?"

"Hmm-mm."

"Can you smell it, the lilacs, and the roses? Can you see the incredible fields of colors that you've never seen before? It's absolutely magnificent. I want you to look up at the sky and see the clouds. And how they start moving and swirling and they start to form a stairway. It's a stairway into the clouds, into heaven, and you're going to climb it. Do you see them coming down towards you right to your feet?"

"Hmm-mm."

"Excellent," I added.

"Yeah."

I continued. "There's a yearning feeling and a sensation that the stairs are for you. There is knowledge waiting for you at the top of the stairs. Go up the stairs and know that it is safe. And you start to climb the stairs through the clouds, the stairway to heaven, and as you're climbing the stairs, you realize that you have no fears. Just relax as you climb and feel excited, looking forward to seeing what is there waiting for you. When you get up to the top, there's a beautiful building just a bit in the distance. It almost sparkles with its radiance. It's absolutely gorgeous. It's a colossal building. You're going to go there. You will see there's a marble stairway leading to large doors. I want you to climb the marble stairway, and as you do, the large doors open as if they've been waiting for you. They've known you were coming. You walk into this grand hall, and there's someone there to greet you. He or she is your guide. Are you in the hall?" I asked as I wondered what information the Hall of Akashic Records would offer her.

"Hmm-mm," she said as she smiled. Her eyes were still darting about, and I sensed that she was visualizing something awesome.

"And what do you see?" I asked hoping she would be very detailed.

"This man is very happy that I'm there. He's very happy to see me."

"What does he look like?" I questioned knowing it was her guide.

"He's kind of stumpy with short hair. I believe he's truly happy I'm here. He's very happy for me."

"I want you to look around the hall and describe it to me," I wanted every detail.

"It's big, there's space all around, a circle from the left with a ring around it that goes forever. There's no end to it. I don't know where it goes. It looks like it from the outside, but when you go inside, it's not like that."

"If you look up, what do you see?" I love this part. The look of astonishment on my clients' faces says it all.

"There's an opening. I don't know how. There's no ceiling. And there are no walls. Lots of shelves. They are there on the sides of the hall," Connie related.

"And what's on the shelves?" I wanted her to focus in on the books.

"A bunch of books."

"What do the books look like?" Every person has a book, and although they are similar in some ways, each book looks slightly different.

"Big, huge books, and they're old, old, worn out books. But they're really special books."

"Welcome to the Akashic Records. You are in the Hall of the Akashic Records. You see that everyone has a book of their life. This is where their book of life is stored. You have a book here, and your guide is going to take you to your book of records, your book of life, your Akashic Records. Follow him and then tell me what you're experiencing."

"We are walking. I am following him." The she corrected herself, "Well, I am walking, but he is floating sort of." Her eyebrows furrowed.

"He is going to take you to your book of records. Are you there yet?"

"No, not yet. He's going all the way down to the bottom to a special place. And now I am going through an opening in the walls, and like going deeper inside. There are more bookshelves here. There's a tunnel of bookshelves, kind of like a secret tunnel of just bookshelves, and it's going all the way back. It reminds me of birth. On the left there's another little tunnel, and that's where my book is. I want to get it. He just gave it to me, my book. He's so happy and kind of proud to be the one who gave it to me. I'm looking at it, and I'm proud of this thick yellowish book. And I feel like a child looking at it. It's exciting." Connie sounded like a kid in the candy store.

"You can ask the book any question you'd like and the book will answer. It has all the knowledge of all your lifetimes, your past, your present, and your future. What would you like to ask your book?" I offered.

"What am I supposed to be doing right now at this time? Will I be helping people? Is there going to be a counseling or healing facility, or service work, or--?" She stopped.

"Just open the book and you will find your answer," I explained. "What's happening now?"

"I just opened the book, and I saw this, all of this life energy is coming out of the book. And it's coming into the air--I think it's coming from something like a picture. I see a forest and mountains. It's beautiful. It's like a fairytale. It's a special place with pastures, forests and trees. I can see lakes and rivers. There are some animals that are so happy there. It's pristine nature."

"Your Book of Life holds all the answers," I explained. "But instead of giving you verbal responses of yes and no, it expresses answers by offering you the experience. This way you still have free will to use the information as you please. What are you doing there now?" I asked.

"There are a lot of people coming to see me, one after the other. It's like a never-ending line, but I don't feel pressured by it all." Connie stopped talking.

I waited to give her time to process what she was visualizing. Then I asked, "And how are you helping them?"

"People are coming to me. I'm going to help God heal them of suffering. They're so sad. Yes, they're sad or broken. Inside, their minds and hearts are broken. They're like lifeless people. I have the energy of a girl that's happy and light hearted. I'm sitting outside on a bench. Each person is coming up to me, and they get on their knees in front of me. I'm amazed at how naturally beautiful it is. Love is everywhere. I take a person's hands, and I hold both their hands together. And then it happens. God energy flows through me and transfers to them.

I understand now that they need to have a conduit. The God energy can't come to that person unless there's a conduit. I get it now. Because they are so dead in their minds, they can't rise up to that God energy, so they need to go to somebody that can pass it on to them. The white God energy is life energy. I just hold their hands in front of them, and I really don't have to say anything. I just have a desire for them to heal, and then the God energy is given to that person, and it goes through their body. I silently smile at the person with love. The God energy starts rejuvenating them, bringing life to all those dead cells everywhere. Then very quickly, that person wakes up fully charged with God energy. Their eyes open wide as they come to life. They're smiling broadly. They are transformed from an almost dead person to someone with new life and warmth with no fear or sorrow or heaviness. It happens just like that in an instant. Then that person looks like a totally different person. They're perfectly healthy with an innocent heart that's so happy and free. They're not sick or heavy. It's so strange. When they leave, they're completely healed. I am so happy to see them walk away. Everyone feels love and gratitude for God's energy. Now there comes another person who's almost lifeless and so broken and gray inside. To go on living like that is just terrible. I hold his hands. I rest his hands on the top of my lap. He's just kneeling there with his head peering down in a lifeless position. There's no joy left in him. I wait for God to put His energy through me into that person. Then it starts flowing into that person's body, and he begins waking up as that energy reaches every cell. Within seconds, he is coming to life right in front of me. He is perfectly healthy with nothing left of a broken heart. He physically appears young and healthy and full of vitality. Now he stands up with his wide eyes and we smile at each other again in awe. He's a new person again. I smile with gratitude and love. It's God energy. Then he walks off, and there'll be another one. That's only the beginning," Connie uttered with enlightenment.

"So you're preparing for this now. You know this is going to come. Where are you located?" I asked.

"It's an unknown place somewhere in the mountains. It's in a preserve or national park that no one has ever been to or where no one is allowed to go. It's got to be special, untouched, or maybe not touched by many. I think it's kept secret, or it's kept private. The public is not allowed to see it or go there. It is in a valley, and there are mountains all around. It's like a fairytale place to live. Other people live there now. Everyone is so happy. There's no sickness there. Everyone is innocent like a child; they're so happy and joyful."

"Is there anyone there that you recognize?"

"Yeah, I see my friend's daughter. She's a teenager, and she has a nice boyfriend and wonderful friends. They're with her too. My mom is there. Everyone has their own separate house. There are many people who live there, but it's a small village. Everybody is busy with something to do. They aren't stressed, but just engaged in work that they're happy to do. They're all doing something special there. Each person has a special purpose."

"Are you doing that in this lifetime on this earth?" I wondered wanting to verify whether she was still in this lifetime.

"Yes. It's this lifetime," she answered,

"Are you ready to come back?" I wasn't surprised when she gently moved her head sideways.

"It's really pretty nice here." Connie didn't want to leave. No one ever does.

"It's time to come back. Close your book and hand it back to the guide," I told her.

"I'm giving it to him now. He's smiling at me with glee. He's really happy for me. I think because he loves doing what he does. Oh, look Jesus is right there. He's standing next to me!" She said excitedly.

I redirected Connie. I wasn't expecting Jesus and there was no way I was going to end the session now. "He's here because he loves you. He knows whom you are, and he has been talking to you for a very long time. Now he wants to come and meet you in person," I said secretly glad he entered the scene.

"It's amazing. He's walking up to me and putting his hand on my head. He wants me to feel his presence. It's a gift for me to connect with him in the physical. He has brought me here."

"Ask him to show you what love feels like," I asked knowing my clients love this.

"It feels incredible," Connie described. She suddenly looked younger as her countenance changed to magical with tears of happiness flowing down her face.

"Ask him what your purpose is here on this earth?" I reminded her.

"Well, that's interesting," Connie remarked, wiping her tears. "My purpose is to help others and not worry about anything. Oh my gosh! My mind is just going a million miles right now! This is amazing!"

"What's happening now?" I questioned.

"He's saying something. He's telling me, 'Now you've seen it with your own two eyes.' He's taking me, and we're walking past the bookshelves, back down the tunnel. There are many tunnels that are secret, and I'm just staying close to him. He takes me to another tunnel, and he guides me again."

"Where's he taking you?" We were well over the time limit for her session, but I wasn't about to stop her.

"He's taking me back to the hall where all the books are. I'm back in another dark tunnel with all the books, and he's standing right next to me. He wants to impart truth to me that's hard to comprehend. He wants me to carefully understand something. I think I understand it. I know what it is. We are all free. We just don't realize it. We simply have to acknowledge that we are free, and then our new lives can begin. He wants us to start now. He wants us to acknowledge that we've been living in the past. We can be free from it now. Isn't that something? We've been following an illusion, and it's like living in a dream only because we believed it is our reality. But the dream has been over all this time. We just don't realize it. The real world has been waiting for us all this time. We just need to realize that. Gosh almighty. Wow, isn't that something? Now he's gently prodding me down the tunnel by myself to return to the place I entered. I think he's happy now that I acknowledged that we've been living in the past. We are all free. We just don't realize it."

"So in your future you are helping others come to this realization?" I asked.

"Yes, I'm walking back to the hall of records. There are tunnels and books. I'm in the back of the hall now. He's standing there, and I wonder how he got there since he was behind me. Maybe he knows of some secret tunnels? We exit through the door, and he hasn't said one word yet. He's just smiling with joy. As we open the door to leave, I say, 'Thank you.' I'm going down the stairs now through the clouds."

211

"Okay. Come back over the bridge and into the garden," I guided her.

"I'm back in the garden. Jesus is with me, and he says it's time to go back up the stairs." Connie began sobbing now at the thought of going back up the stairs. "He's here. He's telling me I need to go back. He's holding my hands, as I think to myself, but it is so magnificent here. He just conveyed to me without words that I need to help others in the physical world, and he needs me to help a lot of other people who need to find him there, too. He's walking with me. We're going up the stairs together. He has my hand. I will help him now. I'll help others attain their understanding. He says that's why you're here. He says I'm here as always, and when you are ready to leave the physical world, I will be here just the same. I'm feeling no separation at all, just like in the garden. People believe that they are separated or disconnected from God, but they never really are. That's why there is all this pain and darkness and dysfunction in the world because people believe there is separation. His father is our father, too. Now I just need to share this understanding about believing what isn't correct. We're never alone. Everything unfolds just as it should."

"Excellent. You are pure energy and have learned a lot today. There are things that you're going to be doing for God by giving God energy to people, taking them from being dead inside to being fully alive again. It's a very important position. You have been given a gift. In a moment, I'm going to bring you back to consciousness by counting from one to three, and when I get to three, you will remember everything and more. You will feel this beautiful, peaceful energy and continue to feel this way forever. This God energy will always be with you. One, you are feeling the chair beneath you. Two, starting to breathe life back into yourself. Three, becoming conscious again, remembering everything, every feeling, and every ounce of love you just experienced. When you're ready to make the changes that you were sent here to make today, you can open your eyes."

"Wow, that's amazing! Wow. Are most people able to go to the Akashic records and have that experience?" Connie wondered.

"Well, I usually take them to the garden during the first session. Most times when spiritual entities enter, like their loved ones, angels or Masters, they usually receive the answers to their questions. If not, I'll guide them into the Akashic Records," I explained.

"Oh my gosh. What I just experienced was so amazing! I can't believe I saw all of that. It was amazing! While I was there, Jesus was just standing there. I didn't need to use words. I just understood it intuitively by connecting to him. It was a knowingness through mental telepathy. The past is an illusion. It doesn't exist. This whole thing is an illusion. It doesn't exist. The stairs were just like the stairs in our physical world. I could see how everyone's perception of things was nothing but an illusion. Their experience looked like this. I could see all the dysfunction, fear, or worry, and stress from each and every individual in the whole world as they were moving about their day. But it was just — it was all an illusion. It was just so clear. I mean, I understood that completely which was amazing. Everyone is just in a delusional dream. Nothing is real. Of course, I believe on an intellectual level that it's probably like that, but to directly experience it is absolutely incredible. I could see it literally. I saw reality as it actually is. It was amazing. That wiped away a huge part of the veil of ignorance of not being aware of this total illusion. We've been wrapped up in it unconsciously without knowing it," Connie described excitedly.

"I follow," I acknowledged.

"I know. Oh my gosh. Well, that was amazing, my goodness..." Connie smiled.

"It was interesting to listen to you. The place in the mountains you spoke of resembled a chapter in your book about how people who should migrate to the north."

"Yes. Jesus says to go north into the mountains. It's critically important. It's a huge part of what he wants to be conveyed in my book. The earth has its own life, and it doesn't like what's happening right now. That really put a new perspective on it for me when he said that to me. It's actually like a being itself, and it doesn't like our presence here any longer because we're destroying it by creating a lot of stress, friction, and negative energy," Connie explained.

"Yes, you hear it on the news every night. It's so much negative energy." I started.

". . . It is. I was blown away when Jesus said, 'Earth will annihilate you if it needs to in order to survive.' And I said, 'Please don't tell me you want me to add this to the book.' And he said, 'Yes.' I said, 'Oh my God,' but I thought for a second. When you are writing a book about communicating with Jesus, how do you tell Jesus, 'No, I'm not putting that in the book!'" Connie laughed.

"I'm sure Neale Donald Walsch was uncomfortable and felt the same way about many of the topics he wrote about. Have you read any of his books?" I asked.

"Well, actually I have. I read the first one when it came out, and I know he has written others. I saw him on Oprah, and I wanted to read the rest of his work."

"Would you explain the work with Babaji that I read about in your book?" I questioned. In Connie's book, she speaks to Mahavatar Babaji, a devotee of Christ and his "right-hand man." I wanted to learn more about him and the healing work he speaks of.

"Basically it's about acknowledging, facing, and feeling an experience without resistance or judgment of your emotional pain. There are many different ways of doing that. There's therapy and talking about it. There's even EFT. Essentially, it is about honoring your suppressed pain and fear. What makes it Babaji's work is that you listen to his mantra, Om Namah Shivaya for about 10 minutes. Either you hear it in a song, or say it to yourself, and that induces the purging of suppressed pain and fear. But it is mainly a process of acknowledging a negative emotion that is most predominant and uncomfortable. It could be fear, guilt, shame, anger, or frustration. Then you sit there and honor it by just giving it a few minutes of your time. Or you can think back to an earlier experience, then an earlier experience, and the earliest experience where you felt the same or a similar emotion and stay out of the story. Stay out of, 'He did that,' or, 'This was horrible,' or judging. It is best accomplished by going into the feeling to feel that specific, negative emotion as fully as you can. You can stay in the emotion until it subsides. It may be ten minutes, or you may be sobbing like a baby for 45 minutes. Then surrender it up to God. Do whatever comes naturally. Sometimes you feel it lighter, and sometimes you will feel it stronger, so he says. You feel a release when you are finished, and then you can continue on with your day. But he recommends doing it daily. You acknowledge and then face things."

"I have my clients do similar work, but I have them journal it. I have them write a letter that begins: Dear Pain, Dear Anger, or Dear Emotion. For some clients, it makes more sense for them to write the letter to important people in their lives. And then at the end of expressing their emotions, whatever is left over, just offer it up their Higher Power to take the pain away. I encourage them to get really angry and release the emotions."

Connie then redirected the conversation back to her hypnotic experience. "I was completely at peace. I was experiencing my true self without the veil of the ego. I have had a similar feeling during times when I was in deep meditation, but this was different. There is a higher state of awareness that's more of a genuine natural state. I think this could be so life changing for people to have this experience even just one time to know that something more exists. That's the whole message of Jesus' second book, Help from Heaven, to know that there's so much more. Having that higher perspective on things helps. This was a surreal experience. It was the first time I've ever experienced total detachment. I had no fear about anything."

"That's a great feeling to have!"

"That's the only thing separating us from having full awareness of God. Once we're willing to face and feel our suppressed pain and release it, we can know God."

"And we can know the Divine State of Mind." We both laughed.

Rats!

"Expose yourself to your deepest fear;
after that, fear has no power,
and the fear of freedom shrinks and vanishes.
You are free."
~ Jim Morrison

Terry came to me looking for help with sleep issues. She had attended Dr. Brian Weiss' seminar a month prior, and she was interested in the possibility that hypnosis might help her sleep. She wondered if perhaps her issue began in a past life since she had sleep difficulties her entire life. Terry had been in traditional therapy for years.

"During the seminar, Dr. Brian Weiss guides his participant into a past life regression. Did you experience a past lifetime?" I asked to assess how easily she goes into a hypnotic trance.

"I did. We did the psychometric exercise and I thought what came to me was absolute nonsense." (This is an exercise when two people exchange a significant personal item to feel and read its energy.) "But," she continued, "it sure meant a lot to the other person. So, I was thrilled about that. And then when we did the session at the end of the day, the regression, I was able to get to the garden, but I didn't find my angel or my guide. I did have a small child appear with very white hair and blue eyes, a little boy, who reminded me a lot of my brother when he was little. And that was it."

"Do you have any idea who the little boy might have been?" I wondered because sometimes if a child was conceived but did not come to term, their little soul shows up in the garden.

"No, but my daughter-in-law is expecting a boy in May. My mother had a miscarriage before I was born so that may have been that child. I had two miscarriages, so I don't know. But nobody in the family has ever had white, white blond hair like that. I was just happy that I made it into the garden."

"Interesting. So I see here you would like to do past life regression. That's wonderful," I said as I was gazing at her intake form.

"I'd like to learn more about myself. I think that it might open up some channels or provide some answers as to the reason I have nighttime anxiety," Terry Explained.

"Okay, so you're having trouble falling asleep. Is that right?" I confirmed.

"That's my whole life." Terry's eyes darted downward and to the right, which is indicative of a person focusing on an internal feeling.

"Tell me about that?" I asked still calibrating her inner emotional state. Whatever was bothering Terry came to her kinesthetically.

"As a kid, I always had trouble falling asleep. That's why I listen to some CD's to try to relax and de-stress and meditate to quiet my mind. I sleep like this." Terry lifted up her arms and crossed them over her face much like a boxer protecting her head.

"You sleep like that?" I had to ask. How could anyone fall asleep in that position I wondered.

"Yes, for protection. I've got a tremendous phobia of rodents, and that is one of the reasons I can't sleep at night."

There it was. Her sleep difficulties could be stemming from a deeper source: her fear of rodents. "So, in this lifetime have you had any issue with rodents?" I wanted to see if the session would focus on a childhood regression or a past life regression.

"Oh, I've had many instances with them. A lot of things that have happened to me involving rodents in this lifetime, but I just can't figure out where it began. So, in my mind I think maybe something happened in a past life, and that's why I feel this way. Maybe that's why my reaction is so crazy!"

"Please explain," I wanted to learn just how crazy she believed herself to be.

"Well, they almost called 911 to take me to the emergency room."

"Oh, I see now," I said realizing that this is a significant fear for her.

"It's pretty bad," Terry added.

"It sounds like you have a fear of rodents, which means you are attracting more rodent experiences into your life," I explained. "When a person has a fear, the universal law of attraction, which is like a magnet, attracts more of the same situations to you. Similar situations come to you to provide you with more opportunities to acknowledge, feel and heal you fears."

"No kidding. I'm like a target," Terry agreed, her head nodding.

"I'm not surprised. It's the fear of rodents that's causing you to attract them," I repeated myself.

"Yes, I feel like I am attracting them."

"The Law of Attraction teaches that you will attract more of whatever it is that you fear. Were you always afraid of rodents?"

"I've talked to my mother extensively about whether something happened to me as a child. Nobody can identify anything specifically and yet, I've always reacted this way from the time I was three or four years old. And it has gotten worse," she added.

"What kind of rodents?" I asked.

"Well, mice and rats are the worst. See, I don't even like to talk about it because now I will dream about it tonight. See my body language has changed already?"

"Yes," I answered as I had already realized it. Terry had pulled back in the chair and was almost cringing.

"I have anxiety," she said as her facial features began to tense.

"Okay," I said making a mental note that she may experience an abreaction during hypnosis. An abreaction is an emotional reaction caused by reliving an experience in order to purge it of its emotional excesses, a type of catharsis. Sometimes an abreaction happens when one becomes conscious of repressed traumatic events. During a trance state, one can go above the situation and observe it as if it were happening on a movie screen without having any emotions tied to it.

"Yeah. I mean it just seems like . . . I've always had this worst-case scenario, worst nightmare situation in my head. 'This would be my worst nightmare if this happened.' And then, a year and a half ago it happened. We were living in our dream home that we both loved. I saw them there. We had to sell the house. I couldn't stay there any longer. I mean when you have to sell your dream house because of it, that's scary. Even after the problem was remedied and proven to be gone, I was still a nervous wreck while in the house."

"Okay, do you meditate at all?" I wanted to change her state of mind.

"I have. I try to meditate at night so that I can calm my mind and go to sleep. Yeah. But recently I've had some horrible dreams again and I just--I mean I wake up in the middle of the night sometimes just shaking and crying and clammy and from a dream."

"I hear you. It must be very frightening," I validated her feelings.

"So, it is just bizarre. It is just, just bizarre."

"No, it's not that bizarre," I said to continue building rapport.

"One time it happened so badly that my husband wanted to take me to the emergency room because I was so distraught and hysterical and losing consciousness from hyperventilating. I went to an acupuncturist the next day, and he gave me this whole tapping thing to do to calm myself. And it helped to a degree. But I know it didn't address the source of the problem."

"I see." Terry was referring to Emotional Freedom Technique (EFT) which is a form of therapy whereby a person uses their fingertips and taps on specific meridian points while talking through traumatic memories, fears, or other emotions.

"It was just a way to try to manage the anxiety," Terry explained, as she looked exhausted.

"There's one way of getting rid of the fear, and unfortunately, it is to go through it emotionally as if it was real and then surrender it. I think that's your biggest issue right now. So, I want to focus on this fear, and, of course, we'll find out where this fear comes from and heal it. How does that sound?" I asked.

At this point, I decided to introduce the HOPE Technique©. The acronym stands for Healing One's Painful Emotions. The HOPE Technique© is a very effectively process designed to heal suppressed pain and fear from past experiences. This technique can be done in the conscious state of mind even though the fear may have originated in a previous lifetime.

No one wants to feel his or her pain and fear initially. But, by harboring and storing painful emotions (energy) from past experiences, new painful experiences are created again and again; perhaps through a different person and a somewhat different situation. But, the same pain or fear will repeat itself over and over until one has faced, felt and healed the negative energy stored within his or her body's cells.

"So, let's set an intention. This is the beginning of the HOPE Technique© to release fear. State specifically what you are upset about," I began.

"I'm upset that I have this fear and phobia of rodents and how it affected my life and others around me to a point that I think is unreasonable," Terry stated clearly.

"You have a fear of rodents. Okay, and exactly how does this affect your life?" I asked.

"Well, it encumbers much of what I do, where I go, how I live, where I live, obviously since we had to sell our house. I couldn't live where I was because rodents were in it. I was acting like a crazy person, having to check everything all the time by constantly looking around me. Any little sound would set me off," Terry answered looking down again.

"Okay. Identify your fear based emotions. You feel . . . fill in the blank. "

"I feel afraid. I feel horrified. And I feel--I've never had anyone validate my fear and my horror until very recently when my outrageous reaction came to such a crescendo in my house. Finally, the only person who has given me some validation is my husband. I would say now my father too because he witnessed my reaction also," she responded.

"So, afraid, horrified, not validated--are there any other feelings?" I asked.

"Persecuted or targeted, like I'm a target, yeah. I feel like I have a big sign on me that says, 'I hate you. Please come to me. Please come and sleep in my bed."

"So, understand the reason you're having these particular feelings is because they are your specific fears. When you avoid and resist feeling these specific fears, they become strengthened. This avoidance behavior creates or attracts more people and more situations into your life that cause you to feel more of these feelings. It's a never-ending cycle until you realize that, and until you feel it fully, and until you accept it. So, now that you accept your feelings of fear tell me when and how this fear has re-created itself."

"A time? There are so many," Terry said as her eyes widened.

"Yes, we're going to go back to them. You can just list them for now."

"Okay. I remember I freaked out at three or four when I saw one in a cage. I remember being tremendously upset. Another time, I was at Girl Scout camp when I was ten years old. We were all sitting in our bunks, and one of the other girls said, 'A mouse just ran under your bed.' I can remember being immobilized with fear. I absolutely could not move, and all I could think was, 'Thank God my trunk is shut to a point where nothing can happen.' Yet every day after that I was terrified to open the trunk. I kept checking to make sure it was closed. I was afraid to go sleep at night. I was afraid not to have my head totally covered. To this day, I sleep like I'm shielding myself."

"Okay," I acknowledged. "Are there any other times that you can remember?" Signs of anxiety were beginning to show.

"I remember going on a picnic with my parents when my father was a teacher. We went to another teacher's house. He was a science teacher, and he had a small lab setup in his house with small rodents in cages. My mom was with me, and she said, 'Oh, we don't want to go in there.' So, we didn't. But as soon as the teacher's son heard that I was uncomfortable with the rodent creatures, he decided to take one out of the cage and chase me all around the yard with it to the point where I was screaming and crying hysterically and hyperventilating. And instead of my father telling the boy to stop tormenting me like that, he said to me, 'Knock it off, this is stupid. Why are you doing this?' This is why I said I've never been validated. I recall another time when I studied at Oxford for a summer. And as I was walking down the path outside the dorm, one ran across it, and I flipped out. I was with a friend and she totally freaked out that I was so afraid because I've always been a very independent, strong person. She just couldn't believe it. And honestly, I'm not afraid of bugs or snakes, or most other creatures. Everywhere I've worked, from my very first job out of college to the last business I owned, I've had rodents in my desk drawers and my immediate workspace as opposed to other surrounding cubicles in the area. Okay? So I'm an expert on droppings. So, I know right away when one has been in my space. I can't go into Pet Supermarket. I can't go into pet stores. I can't go -- I have a friend whose kids had gerbils at one point. I couldn't go to her home. My niece and nephew just got a guinea pig. Since I don't want them to know about my fear, I just avoid going there. I could probably go there if they didn't bring it out, but they're so excited to show it to me that I can't. I had a cat that left a dead one in front of my house one time, and I ran off the driveway screaming in a panic and crying. I called my husband on the phone and said, 'I can't get in the house because this is there.' So, I had to wait for him to come home and take care of it before I could get into my house. While I attended college, I worked at my father's dry cleaning business, and there was this huge field next to it. It was new construction, so I understand the reasons why these things happen. So as I'm sitting there at the counter, suddenly there are three of them staring at me. I ran out into the parking lot hyperventilating to the point where people from the business next door came running out because they thought I was having a seizure or something. They called my father who sent my brother over to close the store. I wouldn't go back in the store for about a week. Every morning, my brother would go in and deal with the traps. It was--I couldn't--I just couldn't stay working there.

It was terrible, and I was only doing it while I was earning my Master's degree. Let me see. There have been so many times and so many places that I had experiences with them. But it was the experience with my house that became my worst nightmare . . ."

Terry went on for several minutes describing her fear of mice and similar rodents. She was so afraid of these creatures that she could not bring herself to reference them by name. I sat there patiently allowing her to tell her story because I wanted her to realize her obsession to give such extraordinary attention to her fear was bringing more of it into her experience. By definition, this is the law of attraction, and I firmly believed she was attracting it convincingly.

She described her worst experience of all in endless detail about her dream house that she ultimately vacated due to her horrifying experiences with these little creatures.

"I'm in the kitchen cooking, and there's one just trotting along in my kitchen like he belongs there. I started screaming, and of course, it runs. So now I'm on top of the dining room table, and I can't breathe. I am crying hysterically, the whole thing. My father wanted to take me to the emergency room because at this point I'm like losing consciousness because I'm hyperventilating and screaming at the top of my lungs and nothing coherent is coming out except, 'It's in my house, it's in my house.' That has always been my biggest fear. It's a whole other level of how upset I get."

After a week of respite at her parent's house, Terry returned to her home after her husband had a pest control company exterminate the entire house. That night, Terry slept smack up against her husband with the covers over her head, terrified. The next morning there were droppings all over her nightstand, which were inches away from her head. The interesting part of her story was that on further investigation, she saw that remnants of rodents were only in her closet, her drawers, and her nightstand. There was no evidence that there were any mice in her husband's closets or drawers. It was her fear, not her husband's fear that mice would be in the house. As she nervously told the story, she was getting herself visibly upset.

The first important step of the HOPE Technique© was for Terry to honor her feelings by giving it her sole attention. It was important for her to not worry about why she was feeling these feelings. She needed to understand that she was completely justified in feeling this fear. I wanted her to feel it – intently, to know how deep this fear was. Ignoring nothing, and just feeling it as deeply as possible by giving it her full conscious attention. Once the fear subsided, surrendering it to Source would be the next step.

It was time to move on.

Terry continued again briefly out of desperation, "Several times a day I have these negative thoughts in my head because of things that automatically remind me of all my bad experiences. And I know it's not good."

"Okay," I interrupted. "So, can you connect the dots to see that it's the fear that is attracting them just as the law of attraction states?"

"Well, I've often said that, and everybody just laughs at me.

"I agree that you are attracting it to yourself. You understand that now," I concluded.

I made a mental note that the rodents were not specifically on her or physically attacking her. Her fear was that they were around her and in her house. It was time for a past life regression.

I started the induction and guided her into a past lifetime. "Let's travel back to the very first time you experienced fear with rodents or rats that may have occurred in this lifetime or perhaps in another lifetime. You'll be very safe, and if you would like to be above the situation just looking down, you may do that as well. That way you can experience and understand what's happening without feeling the fear of it. You will be totally fearless because you'll be above the situation. If you'd like to do that, that's perfectly fine, or if you'd like to go through it and experience it naturally, that's fine too. I'm going to count to three, and you'll be there for the very first time that this issue began. One, two, three, be there. Be above the situation looking down. You're perfectly safe, and you're just observing. You have no emotion tied to what you're seeing. What are you experiencing or seeing?" I wanted to avoid any abreaction she might have.

"There's a wood stove," she began.

"A wooden stove. Are you in your own home?" I asked.

"I don't know."

"Okay. Are you observing from above, or are you in the scene?" I asked.

"In the scene."

"What else can you describe about the scene?"

"There's like an old-fashioned broom. The kind with a stick and wicker pieces tied around it at the base," she was explaining as she moved her hands around an invisible stick.

"An old-fashioned broom. Good. Can you look down at your feet? Are you wearing any shoes? If so, describe the shoes," I asked.

"Black. Black shoes."

"Are you male or female?"

"Male."

"What are you wearing?"

Terry moved her head as though she was looking down. "Baggy pants."

"What color are the pants?"

"Brown."

"And the shirt?" I asked focusing her attention on the scene.

"It's puffy."

"A puffy shirt?"

"Yeah. Dirty white. Not white, white," Terry was now being more descriptive.

"Okay. It's dirty white. And about how old are you?"

"I'm like ten," she answered.

"Is anyone else home?"

"No."

"No, okay. We're going to move very slowly in time. Can you describe what's happening next?" I urged.

"Just the floor is dark. The planks don't all line up."

"Remember, you can always float above the scene. Go ahead, go a little further into this memory. What happens next?" I wanted to approach this very carefully so I could control her emotional state if I needed to.

"I'm just standing here frozen."

"Frozen? And why are you standing there frozen?"

"I don't know."

"Let's move along. We can move forward or backward in time very easily. So, let's go to the next significant event. And what's happening now?"

"I feel like I'm guarding something, watching for something. I'm responsible for it. I don't know what it is. I have to keep the fire going."

"What happens next?"

"I can't move or go anywhere because I have to stay here."

"We're going to move to the next significant event on a count of three. One, two, three. What happens next? Be there," I stated.

"There's a baby in a--it looks like a weird box. And it's just there."

"Is it your brother or sister?" I asked looking for clarification.

". . . In the house," she continued her answer.

"Okay."

"That's why I have to keep the fire going." Terry seemed relieved to know why she was worried about keeping the fire burning.

"Yes, keep the fire going for the baby, keep the baby warm. Okay. Let's continue to the next scene. What's happening now?" I asked.

"The baby is screaming," she announced.

"The baby is screaming. What's happening? Why is the baby screaming?"

"I don't know what to do," she said in a frightened voice.

"It's confusing. You're a little boy," I reminded her.

"I'm looking for somebody to help."

"You're alone?" I questioned.

"Yeah."

"No one is home?" I wanted her to check.

"No, I'm just looking at the floor now," Terry said very agitatedly now. "I'm looking at the stove and the floor, and I don't want to be here."

"Why not?" I asked.

"I don't know. I don't want to do what I have to do. I just don't want to be here."

"What do you have to do?"

"I have to watch her, take care of her."

"And then what happens?"

"The baby cries and cries. I can't find anybody. I'm frustrated."

"We're going to move along. On a count of three, be there. One, two, three, be there. Again, you can always float above the scene, or you can stay in it. What's happening now? What are you experiencing now?"

"They're coming in through the floorboards."

"What's coming through the floorboards?"

"Mice."

"Mice? It's okay. You're safe," I reassured her again mindful of an abreaction.

"I have to get them out!" She retorted.

"You have to get them out? How many are there?"

"Lots of them," Terry answered. The look of fear was clearly pronounced on her face.

"Lots of them?" I asked.

"Yeah. Hundreds of them. They are running all over the kitchen. More and more just keep coming. They are everywhere! They just keep coming."

"What are you doing?" I questioned.

"Kicking them. I'm kicking them out the door." Terry was now kicking her feet in the chair. I could see she was furiously trying to get them out the door.

"You're kicking them out the door?"

"Yes, it's not going well." Terry seemed frustrated, almost crying now.

"It's not going well?"

"No. The baby is crying." She looked and sounded exasperated.

"Continue to describe the scene."

"They're just all over, coming up through the floorboards, and I think I'm not supposed to let them get to the baby. I'm supposed to take care of her. I'm supposed to be watching. I just can't. I can't get them out. I run out the door. I can't find help. I don't want to go back inside. I can't move."

"Are you outside now?"

"Yes."

"Where's the baby?"

"Inside."

"The baby is inside and you ran out?" I asked wanting to know more.

"Yeah. I'm very upset because I know I'm not doing my job. I can't do it. Nothing works. They're all over. I can't do it. I just can't. I can't!" Terry was becoming physically upset now.

"Are you inside or outside now?" I questioned.

"Outside."

"The baby is still inside?"

"Yeah."

"And she's crying?"

"It's crying, screaming!" Terry was becoming frantic now.

"Screaming? What's happening to the baby?" I asked afraid to hear the answer.

"I don't know. I don't want to know. I just want to be out of there. And I don't want to have to do this anymore. I can't find anyone to help me. They're crawling out the door. They're coming like a swarm."

"How many are coming out the door?"

"A lot!"

"10, 20, 30, hundreds?" I asked.

"I don't know! It's just like a swarm. I just don't want to hear the baby scream, and I don't want to go back in. I just want to run away and go somewhere else. I don't want to be here. I'm going to get into so much trouble. I'm too afraid to go back in, too afraid. I can't do it. I don't have a way to make it stop. I can't do this. I don't want to do this, and I'm too scared to go in there. I don't know where to go. I just don't know what else to do. I don't have anywhere else to go. I need someone to help me. I don't have what I need. I don't know where I'll be. I need help, and I can't find anyone or anything. And I just don't want this anymore. I don't want to be here. I don't want to do this anymore. If they bite the baby, the baby will die, but I can't go back in there. I just--I should, but I can't. I hate this. Why did they do this? I don't want to be here in charge. I just want to die. I just really want--I don't want to be here anymore. I just want to die. It's not right. It's not right. I just want to die," she said as she was clearly frantic.

"What happens next?" I questioned.

"I'm running. I'm just running away as fast as I can. I don't know where anyone is. I just want to get out of here. I don't want to stop. I should not be here. I hate this. I want to be somewhere else. I hate this. It's so unfair. I'm so scared. I'm just screaming for help. I can never go back. I can't go back there. I'm so tired."

"And what happens next?"

"I'm resting. I'm in the woods, and I'm just resting. I just have to get away."

"We're going to move to the next significant event on the count of three; one, two, three, be there. Let's go to the time when this is over. Tell me what happened to the baby?"

"I don't know. I never went back. I had to get away."

"Let's move forward to a day or two later. One, two, three, be there."

"I'm sleeping in the woods. I hear birds. I hear water. The river is close. I don't know where I am."

"We're going to go to the next event when you're out of the woods. One, two, three, be there. What happens next?"

"I'm waking up in a bed, but it's not my bed. I don't know where I am. It's somewhere, but I don't know where. My clothes are gone."

"Okay. Let's move forward in time to a week later. Where are you? What's happening?"

"I'm with the horses. I'm happy with the horses. I like this job. I like helping the horses, and I like riding horses."

"What happened to the baby?"

"I don't know."

"You don't know what happened to the baby?"

"I don't know. I just like the horses. I've been walking with them and brushing them. I don't know where I am. It's a town. The horse is my horse."

"Okay. Let's go to the end of this lifetime, the very end, the very last day. You will not be in any pain. The very last day of this lifetime. One, two, three, be there. And what's happening now? Right before you die," I asked hoping the afterlife would give us more answers.

"I'm not well. It's so hot. I'm hot," she said. Her face now flushed.

"Are you ill?"

"Yes."

"Okay. All right, you've passed on. Your soul leaves the body now. What have you learned in this lifetime?" I asked hoping for an explanation.

"I didn't do what I was supposed to," Terry responded.

"What happened to the baby?" I asked again.

"I don't know. I didn't take care of it. I didn't fulfill my responsibility."

"You can see now that this fear is not from your present lifetime. This is a fear you brought forward from your past life, and you can let go of that fear now. You don't have to worry about it anymore. You surrendered your fear to God. What happened back then occurred in a different life. In this lifetime, you have released the fear. It is over now. Do you understand now?" I asked wanting to make it clear to her.

"Yeah," Terry responded quietly.

"We've done a lot of work today. You can relax now knowing this fear was not from this lifetime. It was a thread which has followed you through many lifetimes wanting, waiting to be acknowledged, felt and honored. You have done that today. You have acknowledged, felt and surrendered your fear. When you're ready, open your eyes."

"Wow!" Terry finally came back to a lighter state of consciousness.

"Did that validate your feelings?" I asked.

"Yeah."

"What was most profound?" I wanted to confirm her experience.

"I think it wasn't so much that I was afraid of the rats, but I was unable to do what I was supposed to do because of the fear."

"Right. It prevented you from protecting the baby. You didn't go back because you weren't able to, but you can see now from an adult point of view that you were too young to protect the baby."

"Hmm-mm," Terry mumbled still teary eyed.

"So, it really wasn't about the rodents. It was all about the fact that you weren't able to protect the baby. And now every time you see a rodent, it brings back that fear and that feeling," I responded definitively.

"That's wild. That's really wild. I had such anger that I was left there to do that. That explains why I am always so angry. Why would anybody expect me to do this? I was only ten years old. This explains why I wanted to have all the carpet pulled up in my house and have floorboards put down. I was very adamant about it. I wanted the carpet up. I wanted bamboo floorboards installed. Now, I understand it was because I wanted to be able see if the mice were coming."

"I agree," I said supportively.

Terry was quietly contemplating before she reiterated, "I was left with this baby all by myself? I didn't know how to take care of a baby by myself! I'm just blown away. I keep coming back to those floorboards and the fact that there were big spaces between them. That was really troubling me, and now I understand why. I couldn't understand why it was such a big deal?"

"Is it clearer to you now? You will sleep well tonight," I added in a posthypnotic suggestion.

"I hope so," Terry agreed.

"You don't have to worry about it anymore in this lifetime."

"Yeah. That does explain things. It was something that's plagued me for 54 years. I really felt like that little kid."

"Absolutely," I agreed.

"Thank you so much. That was just mind blowing. I'm still taking it all in. Thank you."

The next time I spoke with Terry she was still ecstatic. Her fear was completely gone, and her sleep pattern was greatly improved to the point where she was laughing in her dreams.

"I was telling my husband," Terry stated with a big smile, "that I had the most hysterical dream last night. He laughed and said, 'Well, that's good. That's a good change.' Then, today I was walking outside, and something scooted in front of me. I really don't know what it was. It could have been a chameleon. It could have been a rodent. I don't know because it was about five feet ahead of me. Normally I would have been a crazy lady, but I wasn't. I just kept walking and thought to myself - No big deal!"

People with fears from childhood or from past lifetimes attract the same situation over and over again because they don't realize that it's the feeling that they're afraid of. The child who feels criticized in childhood has a fear of feeling criticized again. A child who was neglected or feels unwanted or unworthy will attract situations that prompt these same feelings at work, at home, and throughout life which makes him feel that fear again and again until it is faced, felt, and healed. Most people are so used to ignoring or controlling negative thoughts by changing the subject, that they never learn an effective way to face, feel and heal the accumulated pain and fear from past experiences. The HOPE Technique© that I am describing can save a person from a lifetime of unnecessary suffering.

Falling In Love Again

"Once you believe in yourself and see your soul as divine and precious, you'll automatically be converted to a being who can create miracles."

~ Wayne Dyer

Evan's stated intention was to lose weight, gain more confidence and release stress and anxiety. He was finally reunited with the woman of his dreams, and he wanted to feel sexy again. Evan's beliefs concerning his weight were tied to the sadness, verbal abuse, and lack of intimacy he'd experienced in his first marriage. His desire was to become more romantic by feeling healthier and more attractive. He wanted to bring more passion and intimacy into the relationship with his fiancée Lisa.

We began with his beliefs. He believed he was unlovable, unattractive, and undesirable and that no one would want to experience romance with him. Evan began his story.

"Lisa and I dated in the 80s for about three and a half years. We were a great couple, and we had planned to get married at the time. But she became addicted to cocaine. When we first started dating she had stopped using drugs, but then she started using again while we were still together. I wasn't aware of it at the time, but I did notice some big changes in her. She'd be out all night with friends. She kept losing jobs and never had any money. But I thought she might have a mental illness linked to post-traumatic stress disorder from her childhood since her parents had been so physically abusive toward her. I was trying to be understanding by attempting to get her help. I was a 21-year-old kid, and I didn't understand what was going on. Anyway, I was always interested in spiritual learning and spiritual awareness. I tried to get her interested in the things that interested me, and I think that helped a lot. We started attending meditation classes, and we met a meditation instructor who really made an impression on both of us. He told us that he could perform healing by taking you on these meditative journeys. And so I thought, oh, that's cool."

I listened as Evan continued.

"I had some powerful visions during these meditations that were truly amazing. But then the teacher did some stuff with us that was kind of dark."

Evan shifted uneasily in his chair as he described his experience. "This instructor was doing a 'program,' and we did a group meeting with him initially. Then Lisa and I both did separate sessions with him. During my one-on-one session, he told me, 'I need to tell you that Lisa is going to be having sex with a lot of other men. You guys are going to break up, and you're not going to be together anymore.' And I thought we were planning to get married. But he said, 'You guys need to move away from each other.' And although I'd never really cried before, I started bawling my eyes out when he told me that. It was awful. I felt so much pain. Now he's doing the same thing to her. But while he's doing it, he's telling her he can heal her of her pain. She just needs to take her clothes off and—."

"No," I said in disbelief.

"He had her get naked and perform sexual acts with him. It was a sexual experience for him, but not for her. He claimed to be a prominent spiritual teacher, and she was vulnerable. We later found out he did this sort of thing to many women," Evan said. His shoulders dropped and he sunk into the chair. "So, I broke up with her, and I really felt awful about it. She was better off without me. But for her, it was a wake-up call. A voice in her head finally started saying, 'You can't do cocaine. You can't hang out with the people who do cocaine. You've got to have a whole new group of friends or no friends at all.' So she started to replace cocaine with exercise and began getting in great shape."

"Good for her," I offered as Evan sighed heavily. "How did you feel about that?"

"I sunk into a deep depression," his eyes low now as he was looking into his emotions. "I was working six days a week while I was going to college. Then I started drinking to fill the void. I'm not the happiest drunk person you'd want to meet. I was drinking more than I ever had before, and I realized it was too much. I was hanging out with people at work and going to nightclubs every night. Then, a new woman was hired at work. My first impression of her was that I didn't really like her. I saw lots of anger in her. She would yell and throw tantrums, and I just didn't like her. I didn't like that kind of angry behavior. But strangely one day, she asked me out."

"I ended up going back to her house. At first everything was normal while we enjoyed some conversation, but then she started seducing me. She told me she was using birth control and talked me into having sex with her without using protection. It turned out to be a wrong decision. She got pregnant."

I nodded as Evan continued.

"So, now she's pregnant, and she tells me, 'I grew up Catholic.' So, I instinctively knew what she meant, and I thought to myself that I couldn't just walk away and have my kid end up being raised by a stranger or worse - a drug dealer. That's the environment I grew up in. I saw the abuse and the violence that a manipulative person can inflict. My stepfather molested my sister as a child, and she ended up becoming a drug addict herself and getting raped. And, so, I had an immense fear and felt that I needed to protect my child. So, I allowed myself to marry this person. On our honeymoon, she immediately had no interest in kissing, romance, or love. She had no interest whatsoever in sex. All she wanted was money. 'When can I get into your checking account?' She'd ask, 'How much money can I get? Why are you spending money on that? I could use that money for shopping,' she would say. Every conversation was about money. So, I ended up in a nearly sexless marriage while my children grew up. We would have sex occasionally, but it was meaningless and without any real connection. Many years passed without having any sense of romance with Maya despite my honest desire to have more intimacy with her."

"That's sad," I commented realizing the depth of his pain and beginning to understand why he felt unlovable.

Evan shrugged, "I'm telling you this is because this is a big part of what I want to work on. Any time I would try to be affectionate toward her she would say, 'What are you doing? Get away from me. I don't want to be touched.' That's how she treated me. She was a mean, manipulative and hateful person. So, I spent about 20 years with her and during the entire time, my primary focus was to protect my children. She was a very abusive person, and I was constantly protecting the children from her abuse. The experience led me to believe that I'm not attractive. I went from being athletic with a six-pack of abs to someone who was gaining weight rapidly. No matter how hard I tried, I couldn't lose the weight and even now, I am unable to get rid of this," grabbing his stomach roll. "Before when I was with Lisa, I felt a strong sense of romance and intimacy, and I loved everything about women. I had more confidence in myself, and I loved being romantic."

I nodded my head as Evan looked at me. "So what happened next?"

"We finally divorced. Then I bumped into Lisa one day, and I desperately wanted to hug her. But I discovered after all the years of abuse and negative reaction from my former wife that I was afraid to hug Lisa. Even now, I'm uncomfortable kissing or making love. Lisa tells me that I'm not as 'good' at sex as I used to be. And that's when I started to wonder if there was something seriously wrong with me. I know that I'm intelligent. I've got a good career. I've got personal power, although I think that maybe I gave away a lot of that power in my former marriage. So, I've got two core issues that I wrote down on my list of things to deal with. One of them is getting rid of this excess weight. I don't need it. I want to be thin, comfortable, and athletic again. And the other thing that I'd like to work on is becoming a better me, a better version of who I am. I want to become more romantic without fear, because in my heart I'm just a hopeless romantic, and I truly love and adore the essence of femininity. I love being affectionate and passionate with my partner. I feel like I had all these great qualities at one time. I feel like I was a great soldier. I was a great husband, and now I feel like I'm a prisoner of war. I feel as though I was tortured and beaten, and now I'm trying to recover. I must be your worst client ever!"

"No, not at all," I offered compassionately.

After years of sadness, Evan and Lisa finally reconnected, but Evan felt blocked and his self-confidence was completely shattered. This often happens when a person remains in a self-imposed loveless marriage for the sake of their children. After years of disparagement, humiliation, criticism, and no reciprocal feelings of love, it was no wonder why Evan believed that he was unlovable and that no one would want to be romantic with him.

I prompted him to describe his garden to deepen his experience.

"I'm sitting on a bench. There are a couple of benches and a lot of wild herbs like lavender." He took a deep breath to smell the lavender. "And there are fruits, vegetables, and trees, and butterflies," he added.

"The butterflies always come," I said. Butterflies always seem to be fluttering in the inner garden, and when they do, I know my client is in a very deep trance state.

"I feel very happy," Evan offered without being asked.

"Is anyone with you?"

"My stepfather," Evan responded. "Yes, wow, he's so close. And he's happy and very relaxed. I've never seen him like that before."

"What does he have to tell you? You will be able to communicate with him telepathically."

"I'm just saying what comes to me. He's saying he really has a good heart. He really did love us. He's sorry for how he mistreated us. I see him now as a five-year-old boy. He was full of love and happiness; that's kind of how he is now. Everything is great. He says he loves me like a son. He loved my sister and mother too though he mistreated them because he was very hurt. He is saying that I am light. I need to recover and then love gracefully. He has a huge smile. He's so relaxed and happy. I've never seen him like this. I feel him touching my shoulder."

"Yes, and you can feel him. He may want to give you a hug. Would that be all right with you?" I explained.

"It feels like it, yeah —."

"Let him give you a hug, thank him for coming to visit you," I offered.

"I feel all kinds of energy surging through my body."

"He's giving you energy," I said knowing that there is much healing that takes place in the garden.

"Whew. I feel his arms are full of purple light. He just hugged me like a father who really loves his little boy. He gave me a kiss, which feel like true love and real kindness. He said to share this love now. He's fading away."

"Thank him for coming," I suggested.

"Thank you for coming," Evan repeated.

"So, this is the garden we'll be coming to when you visit me," I whispered. "New visitors will come to see you here as well. Are you ready to come back? No?" I saw the reluctance on Evan's face. "I understand. No one ever wants to come back. Why would you want to leave this beautiful place?" I asked.

"I like it here. I like it in the garden," Evan replied.

"I know, everybody does," I agreed.

Evan returned to his conscious state and began speaking. "It's like those videos that show time-lapse photography. Like a plant that grows and blossoms before your eyes in just seconds. That's kind of what that felt like to me. I can feel my heart beating through my whole body like my entire body is beating. It actually feels like love," Evan put his hand on his heart.

"You'll be able to share that love easily now," I repeated what his stepfather said.

"Yeah, it felt like my arms were inflated and weightless, you now, like they weren't really there, and then they just floated upward." Evan was playing with both arms as if they were floating.

"Oh, that happens very often. Many times when my clients are in a very deep hypnotic state, I watch their hands float up a few inches off the chair."

"I didn't expect to see my stepfather," he said.

"Yes," I said, "it's difficult to explain, but you were in a superconscious state."

"And I didn't expect to experience anything concerning my stepfather. I've loved him, and now I've forgiven him, and I'm going to move on—"

"Well, he wanted to come through. He's just the first step in the process toward feeling better," I reassured Evan.

"He was so happy. It was like telling a five-year-old that you're taking him to Disney World, you know. My stepfather had such a profound look of happiness on his face," Evan described.

"That's great," I nodded.

"Wow. What an experience!" Evan said.

We concluded our first session together and scheduled a second session to take place in the upcoming weeks.

At the beginning of Evan's second session, he revealed that much had changed in his life since our last session. He was beaming.

"I see a smile there," I began. "So tell me, what's changed?"

"That last session was really profound for me. As I explained to you during our first session, one of the blocks that I wanted to address had to do with intimacy because I didn't have it for my entire marriage, right? Ever since our last session, my body has been acting more like it did when I was 18. I'm a 48-year-old guy, so that really means something to me. It's one important change that I've seen since our first session together."

I was happy to hear Evan was starting to be able to express himself again, but it was only the beginning of his healing. We began the induction and Evan slid into a trance easily.

"The garden has changed a little bit." He began describing it to me. "It's like the flowers shifted to a different side where the grass used to be and the grass shifted to where the flowers and herbs were growing. And there's a big vegetable garden there now and a lot of butterflies. It smells like orange blossoms, and I see tiny flowers falling off the trees. There are little flowers floating around everywhere. There's an animal, perhaps a deer, off to the left. It's looking at me. It's curious. I feel a lot of movement from many different animals, and there's a lot more life everywhere."

"There may be someone coming to greet you who can help you with your desires. It's someone who loves you very much. It could be a spiritual person, someone who has crossed over, someone who is perhaps still alive or your higher self as well. It may even be your angels or your spirit guides. Is anyone coming to you?" I asked.

Evan was skeptical when he saw his ex-wife in the garden because she is still very much alive. He was communicating with her consciousness, her spiritual essence.

"She's saying, 'I want you to know how I feel.' But I don't know. What is she trying to do?" Evan's eyes cringed.

"Just go with it. Don't try to analyze it. You may communicate with her telepathically. The words just come into your head. There's no talking. The words are just there."

"She's telling me that she has a darkness. She was confused. She is showing me that she almost turned black, or she was filled with darkness. She is saying, 'I was confused. I was hurt by my father. I didn't mean to hurt you. I didn't know how to love a man. I feel badly for how I treated you. I'm sorry. I feel I needed this for my growth.' Now she is adding, 'You are divine,' I was a teacher to her. She's saying, 'I slept with--with other men because I was trying to feel loved.' Now she's turned into a little girl. She's giggling and running into the field where there are flowers everywhere. The field is full of flowers, and she's just running and giggling like a little girl on her birthday. And she's sitting back with me now saying that she wants to feel happy again. Now she's saying, 'I love you. Thank you.'"

"Would you like to forgive her?" I asked. This was for the benefit of my client, not his ex-wife although it may help her spiritually to feel Evan's forgiveness too.

"Yes."

"Tell her."

"I forgive you, Maya." Then Evan became silent for a few moments.

"Maya said thank you. She needed me to teach her. She needed to have a good example of a man so that she could love again and to help her get rid of her anger and her hatred toward men. I just told her that I wish her peace and love, and happiness. She said, 'I will find it.'"

"What is happening now?" I asked.

"'We're both looking at the little girl running through the field. She's the happiest little girl I've ever seen. Maya is looking at that little girl and just smiling. She seems to be searching for the same happiness this little girl has. 'I will find that feeling,' she says. 'I'm sorry I made you feel like you aren't an attractive man. You are a wonderful man, and I won't hurt you anymore.' She says she won't tell the children bad things about me so that they don't have bad feelings toward me. She's going to go find her joy or bliss. And I am too. We don't have a connection anymore. She's saying she will get married before I finish paying all the required years of alimony."

"She will get married before when?" He was whispering, and it was difficult to understand him.

"Oh, she's going to get married," Evan said. "I asked her if she's still going to want this connection to me through alimony payments, and she says she will get married before I finish paying. So, at some point my alimony payments will end,

249

which has been a fear of mine for a long time. She says she no longer wants to have the control or dependency on me because she no longer wants to take from me. She says, 'I thank you for the experience. You looked out for me, how you treated me, and how you raised our kids. You were the man I hoped for, the one I needed.' She tells me, 'You deserve love.' I want her to go away, but she's not going away. Now somebody else just came into the garden. It looks like a woman in a robe. There's something over her head like a halo. This woman is a very loving motherly type. Almost like a Mother Mary. She looks like a nun, but she's not wearing nun's clothing. She's just warm and very loving."

"You may ask her who she is."

"Who are you? I think it's Mary. Yes, it's Mother Mary. I hear Goddess Mother," Evan's eyes widened.

"Don't be surprised. She comes often," I explained.

"I am surprised. My God, I feel overwhelmed. She's leaning over me, stroking my face like a loving mother would do to a sick child. She is so full of love. I feel like I'm going to cry."

"Go ahead and cry," I urged him remembering that he had difficulty expressing emotions.

"Whoa. She's wonderful and all positive. It's like being enveloped in a blanket of love, and it's just overpowering. She's just so calm and so relaxed, and so loving. It's incredible. She's leaning over me, but she's not in a position a human could be in. She's floating horizontally above me. It's like a mother leaning over a child on a bed. She's just looking at me. She's stroking my hair."

A few moments elapsed. Evan was in a state of awe. His face was glowing. "What's happening now?"

"She's floating above me, her hands are touching me in a gentle caress, but it's not on me, it's through me."

"In the spirit world that is how they show you love," I explained.

"I hear the words, 'You are loved. You are loved. You are loved.' She's so warm. Her smile, just the way she is looking at me, the whole feeling is real. I know it is true. She's just smiling and very gently floating back into the field, but very slowly, smiling. She just said, 'I'm not leaving you. I'm never leaving you. I'll always be with you. You'll always have this feeling of love.'"

"You'll always have that kind of love," I reiterated.

"Feeling of love. Now she's in this field right where the little girl was playing before. Mary is just so happy. My ex-wife is now there on the bench, but she looks so different now. She looks thinner and younger. She's wearing pretty, flowery clothes, which she never wore. She only wore black and white, or gray. And she's saying something like, 'I did love you. I do love you. I just didn't have the capacity to allow myself to feel your love. I couldn't express it because of my anger toward men stemming from my father and brother.' I asked her, 'so you had bad experiences with your father? And she says, 'yes, very bad experiences when I was a child. He was angry and hateful.' I tell her that I forgive her. I'm telling her that I no longer have bad feelings or animosity toward her. All the butterflies are fluttering through the air. There are so many different colors all over the place. There's a horse stepping out of the woods and just standing there, relaxed. I think there are some animals in the trees looking at me. I feel like all the animals are looking curiously at me. They're all friendly and harmless. It's as though they want to make friends with me, and they're being patient and waiting for the right time. I don't know. There's a lasso between me and my ex-wife now, and we're taking the lasso off from over my head and I'm gently handing it back to her. She's smiling at me, and it's a warm smile. She's now walking away very relaxed, going right toward the field to the left of where the little girl was. She's almost skipping, just so happy and appears like a girl who was just proposed to. She's happy like a child even though she's an adult woman, probably 30. That's about how old she was when I met her. She seems so genuinely happy. She's just flowing so beautifully with her body movement, and she's slowly disappearing into the tree line. The field is to the right, and the trees are to the left, and she's leaving the garden beyond that tree line along the field. She looking back and waves at me and then smiles and continues off beyond the trees. Now I don't see her anymore. I sense a light coming from along the tree line, like a white balloon with a light inside of it. Pretty birds are flying. And I'm on the bench now. I'm taking a deep breath, and my chest feels lighter. I'm feeling a little sadness though. I feel like I want to cry even though I'm not sad. It's almost like an—"

"--An emotional release?" I asked helping him find the right word.

"Yeah."

"You can do that," I urged again. "Release your emotions."

"It feels like energy, yeah."

"Go ahead," I urged.

"I'm not sure what I am feeling. I feel it physically, extra energy that needs to be released. I want just to push it out, push it out. I feel it needs to be pulled out or something."

"Go ahead," I suggested with no clue what he was now talking about.

"It just needs to be pulled out. I see it. It looks like a yellow rope. It's like those glowing necklaces you get at Disney Land. The rope is filled with yellow light. I have to pull and then open it up when I get to the end of it. Then I need to fill it up with air. Now I am feeling blood from the area. I see red blood or red light."

"Perhaps that was the energy that was keeping you up at night." I was unsure what was going on.

"Yeah, I feel like sleeping. I feel like there's a similar kind of white light moving through my entire body now. It fills me up. It started from my head and flushed through my entire body."

"What flushed through?" I asked, still confused.

"The white light. But it's more than light. It felt like matter. It's hard to describe. It's a dense light, and it's rushing through my body. I can see it in my feet. I'm glowing from it. The color lavender is now covering the field. All the flowers turned to lavender where there was a very light lavender mist. It's very pretty and fading to pink. A cloud is passing through, but it's a cloud of light. God, it's beautiful. This is a very safe place, and I feel very safe. I feel like crying again. . . ."

Evan's first comment when he finally came back to himself was, "Boy, my ex wouldn't leave. She wasn't being unpleasant. But her presence wouldn't leave. I was hoping she would leave. Yeah, she must have a lot of hurt inside of her."

"How do you feel now?" I asked.

"Much better! I think I'm going to have a different perception about those feelings going forward, and I'm not going to let the feelings I had about Maya hurt me anymore. So, I think that's good. Yeah. That spirit was interesting, wow, wow, wow, wow. It was like a silhouette of a person. But you could see the whole person. It was like her body wasn't solid. But that was totally profound. I wish I could draw. If I were an artist, I'd love to sketch what I saw."

I nodded.

Now Evan gazed at me with a confused look. "So I don't understand. Was all of this just my imagination or was this experience part of reality?"

"It always feels like that at first. It is hard to wrap your arms around the concept of communicating with Source. The superconscious state is like a channel or a direct connection to the Divine. In this divine state of mind, we are able to access All-That-Is," I explained. "It is the stepping aside of the conscious and subconscious mind that allows the channel of connection or the stream of information to come forth," I explained.

"You know the spirit thing, I'm a Christian, but I never just felt a special connection to Mother Mary like some people do. So, that was interesting that she came through. That was so powerful. It was all good power. It was very real and very loving."

Evan's third visit started with a very animated conversation. He seemed very happy and eager to tell me what had transpired during the prior weeks after his second session.

"The last time I saw you, my ex-wife and then Mother Mary met me in the garden, which was interesting because I never felt a connection to Mary. I love her, of course, and I have positive feelings about her, but I've always felt a greater connection to Jesus. But interestingly, she came to me. So, that was curious to me. And she hovered right over me, in spirit form. She looked like an outline. I could see her whole body, but it looked like there was just a light mist inside of her. She was filling me with feelings of love and it made me feel like I wanted to cry.

And then when I came out of the session my eyes were watery. I didn't realize it, but I actually did cry. So that happened. My ex-wife came to see me, and I was able to release much of my anger towards her. I feel so much better."

I was happy to hear that. Releasing anger helps my clients feel better, even if the other person knows nothing about it.

"Yeah, and other things--I still have a good job. It pays the bills, but I'm not passionate about it anymore." Evan wanted more out of life. His soul was searching for something more fulfilling.

"What would be the pièce de résistance for your life's path?" I asked.

"First of all I would like to have financial independence, so I don't have to worry about money, and I can just enjoy life, and then I'd like to do something that helps people. I'd like to do something that's creative and fun."

"That sounds interesting." I wondered if I should take him into the Akashic records to see what his life path is, and where this desire to open a spiritual healing center originates. Is this his soul's yearning to fulfill his life's plan? I wondered.

"Yeah, so I definitely want to aspire to achieve that. I have an intuitive feeling that something very positive is going to change career-wise for me this year. And my intuitions have been increasing in the last few months. So, I just go with them," he explained.

"What would you like to know?" Once in a trance, clients often are in such awe they forget why they are there and what questions they want to be answered. For this reason, I generally prepare a list of their questions to prompt them while in a trance state.

"So I'd like to know a little bit more about my past as well as my current path in this lifetime? I feel like I've always been very compassionate to others. I grew up with a mother who just hated me. I felt she'd be happy if I were dead. That's how I felt as a kid. My sister was horrible to me too. She was mom's favorite. We moved every year. We were very, very poor. I was always the poorest kid in school, wearing clothes we got from Good Will that didn't fit me properly. But through all of it, I had a genuine compassion for others, I always have. I was the guy who stood up to the bullies even when they picked on other people. I hate fighting, but I stood up to the bullies. I have an intense compassion for women, and I like to protect them. I also like teaching people. So I wonder if there's something about me or my path that aligns with that," Evan stopped momentarily to take a breath.

"Okay," I inserted.

"I've always told myself that you can't save the world. I always thought it would be great to have super powers and to be a healer, like Jesus. Since learning about Jesus, I always wondered what it would be like if I could perform miracles, and I could alter people's minds, or change their energies. But another part of me would say, 'Evan, that's stupid. You can't save the world. You've got to be rational about what you're doing here.' That was probably the influence on me growing up in a home with alcoholics and drug addicts. So, I just pushed the idea of teaching and healing out of my mind. But lately I've been thinking that it's not such a bad idea. Maybe it's okay for me to have a desire to be able to help people. So, that's my idea of creativity and fun that would fulfill my life's ambition. So, I'm curious to know why I feel that way. I'm starting to think that it's a part of my essence and maybe a role in my future," Evan explained.

I wanted to begin the hypnotic session. "Okay, so let's begin. Close your eyes and relax," I began the induction.

Evan easily moved into a trance state and by-passed the garden altogether. I wasn't surprised. I always have a plan-of-action in my mind, but when my clients get into a divine state of mind, they often go somewhere else and I just follow along.

"I'm outside of a little house. The house is made out of hardened dirt or mud. I don't really see a traditional door. I'm trying to figure out where the entrance is. I think I see an opening like a door, maybe with something covering it. It looks like a cloth or an animal skin. I can't tell."

"Okay. Go ahead inside, and what do you see inside?" I urged.

"It's very dark. There's just not much light coming in at all. There's a room to my right, and it's just dark and very plain. It looks like a storage room. I see dirt and straw and a little light coming from the left. I'm just standing here. It might be some sort of opening with sunlight coming through. I walk further into the house, past the room on the right, toward the sunlight. I gaze ahead, but I sense something or someone is there. I am a little nervous about looking over there, but now I'm trying to focus on that area."

"Look down at your feet and see if they're male or female," I asked to get a better perspective on this lifetime.

"Yeah, female. Yeah, small feet compared to what I have now. And I'm short too," he giggled.

"What are you wearing?" I asked.

"I'm wearing--it's almost like a poorly tailored dress, almost like a robe or cloak or something like a blanket. It is a jacket, almost like a Little-Red-Riding-Hood-kind-of-thing, but not that nice looking. It looks beat up, old, and dirty. There's a pole in the middle of the room, and it appears to be holding up the roof. I'm standing in the center of the house now, and I feel a little nervous."

"How old are you?" I questioned.

"Young, maybe 20 to 25 years old. I didn't feel that when I was walking, but now that I'm looking, that's what I sense. It's like I'm 25, but I feel older. A door is opening in the direction that I'm facing, and now there's light coming in."

"And who is coming in?" I asked.

"It's Jesus. He looks different. He's wearing something over his head, kind of like the cloak that Mary had. It might be cold out. Everybody is bundled up, but, Jesus is lit up. It's as though the sunlight is inside of him, but not the sort of light that would illuminate the room. Now I feel like I'm floating above the scene. Wow, he's very relaxed. He's very happy. I feel the girl's nervousness about meeting him. I think she wants to ask him something. He takes her hand in his hands. He puts his hand on top of her forehead, and he's kissing it. But it's very gentle, and she can feel the energy in her body as every muscle relaxes at once. She feels much love, like when a parent picks up their child to give them a kiss on the forehead. She has a question or a request regarding her child. She's asking, 'Can you help save my child?' I'm not sure what it's about. He's just filling her with love and relaxing energy. She was definitely feeling a lot of anxiety."

Evan was quiet for a bit, and I asked, "What's happening now?"

"He's telling her without moving his mouth that, 'Your child is well, your child is fine, your child is blessed. Your child is happy. Your child is having a great life, doing great things, like he's showing her a child living happily and doing wonderful things for people.' There's a lot of blue light in the house now.

It's a vision to bring us something. He's telling her things without speaking. He wants her to not worry about the child. He's very focused on helping her to not have so much fear."

The scene transformed and now my client was in his body from this lifetime. He was standing in front of Jesus.

"Thank Jesus for inviting you. Ask him what your life path is," I reminded him.

"He's saying, 'You are a healer.' But I don't believe it."

"Ask him how can you best go forth into this lifetime and heal others? What does he want for you to do?" I suggested.

"Jesus isn't speaking. I'll just speak the words I feel that he is imparting to me. I'm just picking up his words," Evan explained.

"Jesus doesn't speak out loud. It's just mind telepathy," I re-explained. "So go with it."

He is telling me, 'Create awareness, open minds, warm hearts, open hearts, relieve anxieties, give hope, compassion and kindness, acceptance.' I'm asking him, 'How I can do this? How can I do this as a career?' And he says, 'Do it every day, all the time, but also as a career.' I ask, 'What career can I go into?' And he says, 'You will have a business, and you will be very relaxed and happy. You will feel no pressure from it.'"

"What kind of business?" I asked, wanting him to have a clearer picture.

"Okay. I'm receiving the words, 'spiritual healing center.' Again, I don't believe it. Where is it going to be? How? And he says, 'A door will open soon.' He says the same words three times. His energy is running through me. He says, 'I will have financial abundance.' But he doesn't seem concerned with that. It's not a business where I'm the owner or boss. It's a collective arrangement in terms of creativity and input. There is intelligence, and energy, and healing. It won't feel like going to a regular job."

"Who are you to open a center with?" I asked.

"Immediately I got the word 'Lisa,' like it was just written on a blackboard in front of my face. I feel like there are others who will help, or be consultants or are involved, or maybe even co-owners or investors. That's a very--hmm, it's not a deal where I'm like the owner or boss. It's a collective energies, at least in terms of creativity and input and intelligence. And there's healing energy --it's good. I feel very, it doesn't feel like going to work."

"Can you see the center?" I asked.

"Yes, I can see something. It almost looks like a restaurant/hotel called the Sunday House in downtown Delray I'm familiar with. It's white. There are trees all around it. It's very natural looking. It's built in the middle of a paradise jungle, or maybe that's just the way it was landscaped. I can't see the whole thing, but it's very large. I'm asking Jesus what to do about my job, and he's saying, 'Just enjoy every moment and help others. It won't last very long.' I don't know what very long means, but he's saying, 'Just enjoy it.' When I look back on this place down the road, I'll enjoy the memories. I'm making a difference for other people right now."

"Ask him if he can explain why you are holding onto this weight?" I reminded him.

"He's saying that a fear of rejection is what's making it hard for me to release the weight. If I become thin and athletic, I can be emotionally rejected and rejected romantically. And my fear is that it can't be because I'm fat and unattractive. I fear that I'm not able to be loved."

"Ask him if he can take that fear from you. What did he say?" I encouraged.

"Yeah, he says, 'yes.' He has a big smile, and he says, 'You are loved. That experience is gone.' I no longer need that experience. 'That experience of being rejected is gone for good in this lifetime. You won't have to worry about that anymore. I will experience the opposite now. I'm experiencing it right now. I just have to allow it to happen.'"

Time was nearing to an end. "Thank him for everything."

"I feel like he's taking the fear out of me. It's everywhere. It's inside all of the cells of my body. It feels like there's stuff coming off all my cells, the inside, outside, every cell. It's like a gray matter in every cell. That's the best way I can describe it, charcoal gray. He just cleansed my body of it, and that will allow the cells to work normally and release the fat inside my whole body. He's saying, 'Use the power of love.' That's a final message he wants me to have. There's a thin beam of light shooting out from him through the ceiling. That same fear tied to weight gain is also the same fear that I have about letting go romantically. I can be like I was when I was younger. He's saying the fear is gone. I just have to be willing to let it go. So, 'Don't hold onto it, or draw it back in, or worry about it because it's gone.' He said she'd have me."

It was interesting that his fear of rejection was keeping the weight on, and the weight was keeping him from feeling sexually attractive. However, his cells knew that if he were to lose the weight, then he would have no excuse should he be romantically or emotionally rejected. In essence, it was safer for him to hold onto the weight as a reason to be unlovable. It was his protective shield.

It was time to end the session. "It's time to say thank you and goodbye. Are you ready to come back?"

"Yeah," he expressed and sounded exhausted.

"I'm going to count down from one to three. So, bring yourself back. One, you are starting to feel your feet and your hands. Two, coming back into your body, back into your mind and you'll remember everything. You will feel wonderful the rest of the day filled with light and love. You'll remember His words of power and love. You will know deep in your soul that he has healed you of your fears of your weight. Your weight may be released now. Your feelings of romance will come back because you'll have no fear of rejection, and you will feel wonderful knowing that your career will be changing soon to a beautiful healing center. One, two, and three, you are now wide-awake and feeling divine." I said as I gave him a minute to come back to himself.

The look on Evan's face said it all. He was awestruck.

Evan was shown what divine love feels like, and now it was up to him to use this experience to learn to love himself unconditionally like Jesus showed him. He hid behind his weight, using it as a reason why no one could conceivably love him. But it was the reverse of what he believed to be true. He needed to love himself first. Just the way he is. Once he accepts himself with all of his faults and learns to love himself unconditionally, then he will be able to let love in from others. Once he stops criticizing himself for his weight and accepts how worthy his is, then the weight will release itself. The cells no longer will have a reason to protect him. They have protected him from years and years of feeling unworthy and believing negative thoughts about himself.

As an interesting side note, when another client of mine was in the divine state of mind, a clearer explanation of how weight acts as a protective shield came through from Source. I thought it was interesting, and so I have included it here:

From Source: Susan's weight issues are not those of food or related drink. The issues are her needing protection, of her not trusting in herself or loving herself enough. Make no mistake, the physical manifestation of weight on the body is always a direct cause of the human needing protection, denying love and life force. All of the exercise and diet in the world will not make a difference if the human is not open to looking at their own unhealed emotional hurts. Susan's hurts go back in time to previous relationships, to issues not yet settled in her own mind. Her solar plexus area is blocking happiness at this time. This is what is not only causing belly weight but also causing blockage to Source messages. What dieting does, dear Susan, is reinforces the belief that something is 'wrong' with you and you need to 'force' the physical body into change. Do you not see the problem this can cause in terms of energy? It is a deep statement to the body, saying 'you are not good enough as you are' and what the body does is respond by protecting itself. The cells 'grab' for protection and this is what adding body fat is – the cells insulating and protecting.

Look on the body for the areas in which the human is carrying weight – you will always be able to see a connection to why it is on those areas. Most, many carry in the midsection due to blocking and receiving love, self-loathing and not feeling good enough. That is why it is deemed so hard to lose from the midsection. It is a very common issue but it is not one that HAS to be an issue. Once you are aware of the cause, you can reverse it quite easily. Susan it would be helpful for you to address your cells in this manner:

"Dear Cells of Mine, I am sorry for the grief I have caused you. I am sorry for forcing you to carry my negative thoughts and to carry more than I needed. I love you, and I am letting you know that you no longer need to carry negative thoughts anymore, about myself or my body. You need the break from this, and I'm sorry for not realizing this load I was placing on you. From now on, only loving thoughts will be carried, and I will tell you daily how much I love you and appreciate all you have done for me. And I will love you always exactly as you are, exactly as you are this moment in time, forever. You are worthy and lovable exactly as you are!"

Believe this Susan - once your body realizes you love it, that you do not hate it, that you accept it and appreciate it for all it has done, the cells respond immediately in loving fashion. Worry not about strict diets as they never ever work anyway. Depriving yourself causes resentment, anxiety and those are emotions no one needs when trying to lose excess weight. What they need, and what most deny themselves of, is love and acceptance for this is all that is required for the body to turn and release all the extra weight.

Evan smiled and said, "I'm very pleased with the session. So, wow. This is amazing stuff, Susan. Sometime I might ask you who you really are."

"Who I really am?" I asked.

"Yeah."

"I'm just the guide," I said.

"Yeah?" He said with a disbelief in his voice.

"It's all there for you. I'm just the guide."

CONCLUSION

"What is is - and whatever is, is our teacher!"
~ Gloria DeCola, a.k.a. Momma Gloria

And guiding people is precisely what I do. Where they go while in their divine state of mind is entirely driven by their spirit consciousness. Listening carefully to my clients allows me to plan our session to deal with their particular needs, however, in the end, Spirit knows best. I follow along and guide my clients as best I can with confidence that the perfect experience will unfold and manifest their healing.

It has been a remarkable journey, and I am happy to have been a part of each client's experience. I never imagined that studying hypnosis could produce such spiritual encounters, but I am glad for the outcome. I have always heard the expression, "One's mind is a curious thing." I just never knew how curious it is indeed.

The subconscious mind is a storehouse of memories, and we are able to access it by simply quieting our minds and relaxing into it. Infinite wisdom is available to us all through the superconscious mind, we just need the key to open this door. Through one of my clients, Source revealed how to open this gateway to this communication.

From Source: "The superconscious is your direct connection to the Divine. It goes beyond what is even subconscious in your human mind. Bypassing the subconscious takes you to a state of true freedom, true release -- with no ties to the human body form in any way. This may sound frightening to some, or as if you are accepting death. However, there is no death. The clear connection to all of that is Divine is through the superconscious. The subconscious, however, is a step to getting there. It is not to be dismissed, as the subconscious is also very important. It is in the state superconsciousness that all are able to access All-That-Is, every form of creation that has ever been in existence. For this is the true sate of your being, where you originated from and where you will all be again and again as you decide on which new journey to embark on as a soul."

Limiting beliefs block our capacity to transcend our earthly existence, but as witnessed through my work, it is possible for anyone to understand the origins of their thought process. Our minds contain the essence of our nature through experience. Napoleon Hill appropriately said, "Think twice before you speak, because your words and influence will plant the seed of either success or failure in the mind of another."

The distant past can purposefully whisper into the present and result in many unexplained fears, phobias, emotional pain, and suffering. Prior lifetimes that we've shared with the souls of people whom we know and interact with in our present lifetime can explain the horrible relationships we develop. Of course, the opposite can be said as past life experiences can also shed light on the beautiful experiences we share as well.

It is fascinating to understand how we can build metaphorical concrete walls, create invisible shields, or gain extra weight just to protect ourselves. We protect ourselves so instinctively, and we can live an entire lifetime trying to shield ourselves from being hurt. And sadly, we lose sight of the one thing we are here to learn and experience most of all - Love.

In the end, it is only fear that keeps us from knowing who we truly are. Fear of getting hurt, fear of feeling rejected, fear of the unknown, fear of death, the fear of being unloved, unworthy, or unappreciated. These are real fears that people cope with every day. There is only one way to find freedom from fear and experience who you truly are and that is to acknowledge your fear and face it head on. Once we acknowledge and face our fears, they will disappear. What we resist will persist. Remember, the only real fear is our fear of being separated from God, our true Source. And since fear-based experiences are just an illusion, you can safely let it go and find peace, happiness, and love.

For more information or to schedule a hypnosis session with Susan, go to www.GetJoyful.com. Skype and in person sessions are available.

More information about the HOPE Technique© (Healing One's Painful Emotions), a tool given from Jesus for effective emotional healing, may be found at: www.DivineUniversity.org.

Made in the USA
Charleston, SC
02 April 2016